THE TWELFTH ANGEL

• THE •

Twelfth Angel

OG MANDINO

FAWCETT COLUMBINE
NEW YORK

A Fawcett Columbine Book
Published by Ballantine Books

Library of Congress Cataloging-in-Publication Data
Mandino, Og.
The twelfth angel / Og Mandino.—1st ed.
p. cm.
ISBN 0-449-90689-2
I. Title.
PS3563.A464T84   1993
813'.54—dc20   92-54995
CIP

Manufactured in the United States of America

First Edition: May 1993
10   9   8   7   6   5   4   3   2   1

In loving memory . . .

Doug Turno

. . . the bravest little
guy I've ever known
&
Rev. Jack Boland

. . . the bravest big
guy I've ever known

A HUMBLE ACKNOWLEDGMENT

This book could have never been written without
the help and guidance of my son, Matthew. The
story line for *The Twelfth Angel* came from Matt as
well as the good counsel and advice that I needed
in order to do justice to this very special tale.

Og Mandino

Everyone's life is a fairy tale, written by God's fingers.
—Hans Christian Andersen

THE TWELFTH ANGEL

I

*S*olitary confinement.

Self-imposed.

For many days after the funeral I did little when I was out of bed except slump at my desk in the den for countless hours and think about ending my life. The phone was off the hook, fax machine disconnected, and all doors leading to the outside world were locked and bolted. Still, each day, what seemed like an endless stream of traffic had moved slowly up my long circular driveway, always followed by a mournful tolling of the door chimes until I finally ripped out some wires. Sympathy from my friends and neighbors was the last thing I wanted.

The past seventeen years. How special they had been. Filled with hard work, rewards, love, joy, success, achievement, laughter and even some tears. There had been so many precious moments, such a long run of proud and unforgettable experiences, and now, even before my fortieth birthday, life was suddenly no longer worth living.

Occasionally I would push myself away from the desk, rise, and move slowly around the room, pausing to stare at each of the framed family photographs on my walls. Memories. The good times and special occasions depicted in each picture were still so vivid to me that I could almost hear voices and laughter. Was it Lord Byron who wrote that we can see farther through tears than with a telescope?

I turned my high-back wooden swivel chair slightly to my right, reached down to the bottom drawer of my large oak desk, tugged at the handle and it slid open silently. Inside, resting atop a telephone directory and several seed catalogs, where I had placed it yesterday after a long search through still unopened packing cartons in the garage, was the dull-finished .45-caliber Colt automatic pistol that I had bought, secondhand, during a rash of house burglaries back in Santa Clara, ten or so years ago. Next to the old weapon was a box of cartridges, a full box. I hated guns, always have, and after three test shots in the basement of a San Jose gunshop, I had never fired the damn thing again. Now I placed the lethal instrument on my desk blotter and stared at it, running my fingers slowly along its scratchy surface. On the flat side of the barrel, just above the trigger, was the small outline of a rearing horse and the words *Government Model, COLT, Automatic Caliber .45*.

I raised the muzzle end of the gun with thumb and forefinger, stared down the barrel and despite my shattered state of mind a name suddenly flashed through my self-pity to add to my confusion—Ernest Hemingway. *Dear God! A ghost from my childhood!* I had discovered Hemingway's books in the local library when I was ten, and that summer I devoured everything of his I could find. It was after reading *For Whom the Bell Tolls* for the second time that I made my decision. When I grew up, I would be a writer, a famous writer, and I would find adventure in all parts of the world like Hemingway. What a wonderful life that would be! And then . . . and then my hero let me down. One day in 1961 he placed the business end of a loaded shotgun to his head and pulled the trigger. I had a terrible time dealing with that. Why would anyone be foolish enough to do such a thing? Why? No rational answer came from the grown-ups I queried. Why? Why? What could possibly cause a man to take his own life, especially a big, tough, smart guy like him—a man who had so much to live for? I leaned forward and peered down the gun's barrel again, shaking my head as my eyes filled with tears. *Mr. Hemingway, please forgive me for judging you and thinking you were dumb to do what you did. Please.*

I turned my back on the gun and gazed out the picture window directly behind my desk. Just below was a wide deck that extended across the entire rear of the new Cape Cod–style house. Rolling slightly uphill, away from the deck, were several acres of dark green lawn, studded with white Adirondack chairs, a horseshoe court, cedar picnic table and benches, and two six-foot-tall golf pins with red practice flags, set approximately a hundred and thirty yards apart so that I could practice with my short irons. At the far side of the lawn was a long single row of newly planted privet hedge, and beyond them was a meadow with several huge granite boulders, tall blueberry bushes and a small pond filled with noisy green frogs. Behind the meadow was a stone wall and a thinned-out woodland of pine, birch, maple, and a few ash, extending to both my left and my right as far as I could see. Raindrops suddenly began to fall, splashing against the window and diffusing my view until the outside world through the glass looked more like a painting by Monet. Forty-four acres of heaven on earth. Sally and I had fallen in love with the house and grounds at first sight. Bought it the very same day the realtor showed it to us.

Sally . . .

I was now sitting in almost exactly the same position as on that Saturday, just a month ago, when she had walked into the den, stepped around my desk and hugged me. "Well, hometown hero," she asked proudly, "are you ready to greet your public?"

"I'm not ready but I am nervous. Hon, I haven't seen most of these people for a lot of years. I can't believe this old town is doing this."

"Why shouldn't they? The people of Boland are very proud of you, John Harding. Your mom and dad spent their entire lives in this community. You were born here, went to school here, were a three-letter man in high school as well as president of your senior class, went on to college and became a baseball All-American. Now, here you are, just twenty years later, moving back to your hometown while you are being acclaimed by the entire business world as the newly elected president of Millennium Unlimited, one of the largest and most powerful computer companies in the computer industry. And ... and ... you're still so young! Why shouldn't these people honor you? Real heros are getting tougher and tougher to find in this crazy world of ours, and this town of Boland, as well as the rest of New Hampshire, has every right to pay tribute to you and all that you have done with your life. In the past few weeks most of them have seen you on *Good Morning America* or the *Today* show and read about you in *Time* and now they can't wait to see you in person, especially the old-timers who knew your folks and remember you as a little boy. I was chatting with a Mrs. Delaney down at the post office this morning and she told me that the town hasn't been in such a frenzy since Commander Alan Shepard, from Derry, dropped by for a clambake supper after he had become the first American in outer space—and that was almost thirty years ago!"

New Hampshire was a completely new experience for Sally, whose roots were all in Texas. We were both recruited out of college by a Los Altos firm that manufactured portable adding machines. Three months after we met, we married. Smartest thing I ever did in my life. In the years that followed, we probably moved our skimpy collection of furniture and clothing six or seven times up and down what would later become known as Silicon Valley as I kept changing companies in my persistent climb up corporate ladders. Sally was a rarity of the age. She insisted that all she wanted to do was stay home, be a housewife and mother—and my cheerleader. She was all of those and more to me, and seven years ago we were blessed with a healthy son, Rick.

Just two years ago I had assumed the vice-presidency of sales for Vista Computer in Denver and after I was fortunate enough to double the company's dollar volume, both years, I was approached by an executive headhunter for the position of president of Millennium, third largest manufacturer of computer software in the world. The board of directors, it seemed, had voted unanimously, after two years of decreasing sales volume, to go outside the company for leadership. It was a dream come true for me, both the opportunity to head my own company and also to return to my New Hampshire roots.

Since the company's headquarters and main plant were in Concord and my old hometown of Boland was only about a thirty-minute drive away, on good roads, Sally and I decided to look for a home in Boland, and we got lucky. Of course our West Coast furniture was completely out of place within the traditional architectural styling of the new rooms, but that didn't faze Sally a bit. Almost overnight she was deep into books and catalogs on early-American and colonial interiors and she solemnly assured me that before we had our first house party for Millennium's executives, our new home would be furnished in a manner that would make even Paul Revere proud, providing we didn't run out of money first.

"Well," I sighed, after Sally had finished singing my praise, "they said they wanted us down on the town common at two, so I think we had better get going. Where's our son?"

"Rick is in the living room, sulking. He's not very thrilled about his usual Saturday afternoon baseball game with his friends being fouled up by adult doings, but since it's his birthday next Wednesday, he's struggling hard not to lose any points."

I grinned. "Well, let's go take our bows and get on with our lives."

~~~

II

I remember so vividly the rare sight of heavy traffic on Main Street as our Town Car inched past automobiles parked on both sides of the recently tarred pavement on that Saturday morning. Drawing closer to the common, we began to hear the brass and drums of a marching band.

The township of Boland, population five thousand plus, founded in 1781, was such a typical small New England community that it almost looked like a Hollywood set. Along its two-lane, maple tree–lined main thoroughfare were three old spired white churches, one small restaurant, a grocery and hardware store, police station and town offices sharing the same aging red-brick building, a Grange hall, two filling stations and a branch bank. Not a single new building had been erected along the town's downtown "business" district since I had gone off to college in '67, and only a huge stone foundation remained, now nearly covered by weeds and brush, from a fire four years ago, that had totally leveled the Page Public Library, my favorite hangout as a youth. That spacious Georgian-style building had been erected through a generous bequest from one of Boland's most successful citizens, industrialist Colonel James Page, and his gift to the town had also included sufficient funds to fill all the library's shelves with books. Unfortunately neither while the edifice was being erected nor in all the years it had served the people of Boland had any of the town's officers ever thought about making arrangements to insure their most beautiful municipal building, and the small town, despite several attempts, had never been able to raise the necessary funds to rebuild after the fire. Across from the library ruins was the bench-lined common, and at its northern site stood the bandstand with a new coat of light-blue paint.

"Wow," exclaimed Rick as he leaned closer to the front windshield, "look at the crowd of people, Dad! Are they all here for us? If they are, can I please just stay here in the car and wait for you two?"

I pointed ahead at the banner that hung tautly across Main Street, WELCOME HOME, HARDINGS . . . BOLAND IS PROUD OF YOU! "See that, Rick? That greeting includes you, fella!"

My son tugged at his baseball cap and puckered his lower lip. "Why me? I didn't do nothing."

"Well . . . you are a Harding, right?"

"Yes."

"Then you are an accomplice. You're in this with us."

A uniformed police officer standing close to the side-walk near the commons began waving his arms frantically as soon as he spotted my car. He gestured toward an empty parking space that he must have been saving for us. As we stepped from the car, to loud applause and cheers, the officer raised both his arms protectively. "Welcome, folks. Will you three kindly take each other's hand and follow me closely to the bandstand? Please don't stop to greet old friends during this trip, because if you do, we'll never get to that platform before sunset. There will be plenty of time for all that later, but right now they need you up there," he said loudly as he nodded toward the bandstand. The townfolk were sitting so close to each other on the common's newly mowed grass that many had to stand in order to make room for us, but with the officer's help we finally did reach the bandstand's steps, where we were greeted by a smiling man with a huge crop of white hair.

"Welcome, John," he shouted above the band's rendition of "Hail, Hail, the Gang's All Here!" "I'm Steve Marcus. Don't know if you remember me but—"

"Steve, of course I remember you. Our class treasurer, played left field your junior and senior year . . . and I heard you now have your own law practice in Concord. You look great and haven't changed at all—except for the color of this . . ." I said as I ruffled his hair.

On the bandstand, seated in a half circle of wooden folding chairs, were the other guests. Steve walked us down the row, introducing Sally, Rick and myself to the three town selectmen, the fire chief, police chief, high school principal and the pastors of the town's three churches. I knew none of them from my early days except one of the selectmen, Thomas Duffy, a retired judge who had been a good friend of my dad's.

"John," he said in his fondly remembered basso-profundo voice, "my only regret is that your mother and father are not here today to take part in this very special occasion."

"Mine, too, sir. Judge, you are looking just great!"

"And so are you, son, so are you."

Steve paused before the next chair but made no introduction. Instead, smiling slightly, he asked, "Do you remember this lady, John?"

I leaned closer. She was a tiny woman, wearing a delicate summer floral-print dress, her silver hair pulled back tightly in a bun, a small white-cloth handbag resting on her lap. She looked up at me almost timidly, through rimless glasses, and there was a slight quiver in her lower lip as she moaned and reached up with both hands toward me.

"Miss Wray," I gasped, "is it you?"

She closed her eyes and nodded. I knelt down to embrace my first-grade teacher, that special person to whom I owed so much because she had instilled in me a passion for books that had contributed toward every step I had been able to take up the ladder of success. I kissed her cheek gently and said, "Now this truly is a special day!"

Miss Wray nodded while tears ran down her wrinkled cheeks. After I had introduced her to Sally, she motioned toward Rick and asked, "Is this your son, John?"

"Yes. This is Rick, Miss Wray. He'll be in the third grade this fall."

"Rick," she said in a firm voice, placing her small hands over my son's, "I hope that you are as proud of your father as we all are. We knew, even when he was very young, that he would be an important person someday."

Rick finally found his tongue and asked, "Did you really and truly teach my dad when he was only in the first grade?"

"I certainly did. Almost thirty-five years ago."

"Was he very smart when he was little?"

Miss Wray nodded vigorously. "If I could have promoted him directly into the third grade, I would have done it. That's how smart he was!"

I felt a hand on my shoulder. "Sorry to break this up for now," Steve said apologetically, "but everyone is ready to start the program. John, you and Sally and Rick take those three empty seats in the center and we'll get started."

First we all stood and sang "The Star Spangled Banner" accompanied by the Boland High School Band in its familiar uniform colors of maroon and white. Then one of the clergy gave a brief invocation followed by a buxom woman with a lovely voice singing the Streisand classic "Memories" while I held my wife and my son's hands very tightly, thanking God again and again for all my good fortune.

Judge Duffy then rose slowly, walked to the microphone with no introduction, tilted the instrument slightly upward, cleared his throat and said, "Ladies and gentlemen of Boland, this is indeed a special chapter in the history of our old town as we gather here to honor one of our own for all that he has made of his life in such a few short years. I am most proud to say that I was a friend of Priscilla and Leland Harding. I can remember when John was born and how proud his dad was when we met outside the bank and he shoved a cigar into my shirt pocket. Leland's pride in his son would have multiplied through his later years had he lived. John was an all-star shortstop in the Boland Little League, he was a member of the National Honor Society and he graduated from Boland High with straight A's. During his senior year he captained both the football and the baseball teams and was an all-state forward in basketball. Also, during his senior year on the baseball team, his batting and fielding were so sensational that he won a scholarship to the college with perhaps the finest baseball program in the nation, Arizona State University. During his senior year at Arizona State, John was batting more than four hundred and had major-league scouts drooling before torn knee cartilages sadly ended his dreams of a big-league career. . . ."

Main Street had obviously been closed to traffic as soon as the program had commenced, but what amazed me, as I sat and listened to Judge Duffy, was the behavior of the huge crowd. Except for an occasional cry from a baby, everyone was, or seemed to be, hanging on the judge's every word. I wasn't sure whether they were captivated by his marvelous oratory or my record.

The judge continued, still without referring to any written notes. "As broken-hearted as John Harding was when his baseball-playing dreams came crashing down, he still graduated near the top of his class in 1971, was recruited by a California high-tech firm and now, in less than twenty years, he has certainly made it to the major leagues in the business world! As most of you know, our beloved young friend was recently selected to become president and chief executive officer of a computer company, perhaps the largest in New England, with annual sales of more than a billion dollars—that's a thousand million, in case you've forgotten your high school arithmetic, folks! The media, from our own *Concord Monitor* and *Manchester Union Leader* to the *Wall Street Journal, USA Today* and *Forbes*, have all joined the loud chorus singing the praises of John's managerial style as well as his character. If you have had the pleasure of seeing him on national television recently, you cannot help but like as well as respect this bright young man. However, what makes me most proud is that when John came east to assume leadership of his company, he chose this town as the place where he wanted to settle with his family. Oh, he could have selected many high-fallutin' communities around Concord, but he picked Boland. He's home again, right back on the land where he spent so many happy years growing up, back with the people who remember him and still love him!"

While the applause grew louder and louder, Judge Duffy turned toward me, smiling as he reached into his jacket pocket and withdrew what seemed to be a large bronze medal dangling from a wide red ribbon. "John Harding," he said in his best courtroom voice, "would you kindly come forward to receive a small token of how these good people feel about you?"

The medal was at least three inches in diameter. The judge held it close to his face and said, "On this medal are the words, 'To a favorite son, John Harding. Boland is truly proud of you.' Our town seal is on the other side along with the state's motto, 'Live free or die!' " He held the medal high above his head as the crowd roared, turned and draped the red ribbon around my neck before embracing me. Then he limped slowly back to his seat.

The people had risen to their feet, applauding and cheering, and the band suddenly began playing "The Impossible Dream." I turned toward Sally. She was crying, but Rick was standing and applauding. I just stood at the microphone until the music ceased and the crowd quieted down.

"Friends and neighbors," I began as I tucked the heavy medal inside my sweater to prevent it from banging against the microphone. "I thank you from the bottom of my heart for this warm and very special gesture of love toward myself and my family. Also, I deeply regret that even though we have lived among you now for almost two months, I have been so busy in Concord, taking over the reins of Millennium, that I still haven't had time to visit with many old friends from the past, and I beg your forgiveness. I shall correct that omission as soon as possible. Before too long, I promise you, the Hardings will throw the barbecue to end all barbecues at our home, and when we do, all of you are invited!"

I waited until the cheering subsided. "One of the things that has amazed me since my return is how many of you have never left Boland. You were born here, grew up here, went to school here, got married—and now you're raising your kids here. How wise! You all know a good thing when you see it. I cannot think of a better environment in which to live a happy and peaceful life than right here, in the heart of New Hampshire.

"Like Judge Duffy, I, too, wish my mom and dad could have been here to share this special moment with us but . . . but . . . I'm sure they are watching, just as I am certain that I could have accomplished very little without their love and guidance. I thank you all for coming. This day is without doubt the highest point of my life."

And then, only two weeks after the celebration, my life plummeted from its peak to the utmost depths of anguish and despair. Sally and Rick were on the Everett Turnpike, going south to Manchester to do some shopping, when an old Ford pickup truck, heading north, suffered a blowout of its left front tire, careened across the center strip of grass and struck Sally's station wagon head-on. Both Sally and Rick were killed on impact. . . .

. . . I don't remember how long I had been staring out the rain-streaked window in my den before I turned back to the desk and the Colt .45. I opened the lower-right desk drawer again, removed the box of cartridges and placed it next to the weapon. Then I tipped the container until several ugly-looking brass cartridges rolled toward me. This was it. I wanted to die. Very much. I wanted the pain in my heart to stop, and there was no medicine available anywhere that could relieve my agony. Living without Sally and Rick was a punishment I did not have to endure a moment longer. I removed the empty cartridge magazine from the pistol and began stuffing bullets into it. Easy. Finally I was ready. I shoved the magazine back into the gun. *Hurry! Don't think about it! Just do it!* I raised the gun to my forehead.

"Dear God," I sobbed, "please forgive me!"

And then an angel—yes, an angel—saved my life!

III

At first it sounded like distant thunder. When it persisted, in an almost rhythmic beat, I realized that the thumping sounds were being made by someone pounding on the rear of the house clapboards. Then I heard footsteps on the deck and a voice shouting, "John . . . John . . . are you in there? Answer me, please. Open the door, any door . . . even a window! John, it's Bill West. Can you hear me, old buddy?"

Bill West? Could it be? He had been my closest friend during all the growing-up years in Boland, as close as any blood brother could have been—from that first day of kindergarten when two frightened little boys shared the same seat in an old yellow school bus to our double-dating in his dad's green Buick for our high school senior prom. Bill West? Bill West? My comrade, teammate, fellow Boy Scout, confidant and alter ego. Was that re-

ally Billy's voice calling me from my deck? Even before
Sally and I began our house hunting around Boland, I
had tried in vain to make contact with him. Eventually
I had learned that although he still lived in town with
his wife and two sons, he was in Santa Fe, on a three-
month sick leave from his company, recuperating from a
triple-bypass operation that had almost killed him.

The sound of pounding grew nearer and louder.
Quickly I jerked open the desk's right-bottom drawer,
dropped the pistol and cartridge box on top of the
phone book and seed catalogs and slammed the drawer
shut. I certainly didn't need any witnesses to my suicide,
especially my oldest and dearest friend.

Suddenly there he was, peering in my picture window, his hands shielding his eyes, yelling, "John . . . it's
Billy West . . . answer me, please. John!"

I stood and moved close to the window. Bill staggered
back several paces before he recovered his composure,
grinned and pointed at me. "Hey, old buddy. Finally
found you! It's me, John. . . . Bill . . . Bill West!"

I forced a smile and then motioned for him to come
closer to the window so that he could hear me. "There's
a door down at the end of the deck," I yelled, pointing
to my right. "Go on down there and I'll unlock it for
you!"

We embraced for several minutes and then stepped
back but not so far that we released our hold on each
other. The palms of Bill's two hands were patting my
cheeks while my fingers were locked tightly behind his
neck. We were both crying.

Bill spoke first after removing a handkerchief and blowing his nose. "Hell of a reunion, isn't it? I'm so sorry, John."

I tried to answer but couldn't. Bill placed his hands on my shoulders and said hoarsely, "I had read all about your big move up to Millennium. Aunt Jessie phoned us in New Mexico to give us the news about Boland's planned welcome-home celebration, but my doctor insisted that if I truly loved my family, I should just lie around in a hammock in Santa Fe for another couple of months before coming back. He said I could celebrate with my old friend later. But when Jessie called again with the terrible news about Sally and Rick, I couldn't stay out there."

"Bill," I said softly, "you should have listened to your doctor. Thanks for caring, but there's really nothing that anyone can do for me, I'm afraid. Hey, let's not stand out here. It's a lot more comfortable in the living room."

We sat in silence until Bill finally said haltingly, "It's a . . . a . . . lovely room, John."

I stared down at the antique Heriz carpet and shook my head. "Sally kept promising me that by Christmas she'd have it looking just the way we wanted. I think I've only come in here once since the accident, and even then I could only stay a couple of minutes. My pretty lady is everywhere I look. I can remember the afternoon we bought that Queen Anne armchair and walnut slant-front desk in Conway and the rainy Saturday morning when we were shopping for vacation clothes and came home with this Chippendale sofa instead."

Bill looked around the room slowly, pausing to study the oil painting of clipper ships sailing in Portsmouth harbor, the Shaker rocking chair with woven-tape seat, the oversize fireplace with its carved walnut mantelpiece and flintlock rifle hanging above its shelf and the eight-foot-tall grandfather clock in the corner nearest to us.

"Magnificent," he sighed just as the clock chimed the quarter hour.

I nodded. "Sally's favorite . . . of all the furniture."

Bill forced a smile. "How long has it been since we've seen each other?"

"High school reunion. Our tenth, wasn't it? I only came for that one. Then I got too busy."

Bill shook his head. "That's a dozen years ago! Where the hell is the time going?"

"Old buddy, I don't know . . . and I really don't care."

"They tell me that no one has seen you around town since the funeral. Have you been locked up in this house all that time?"

"No. Every night after dark I walk down the driveway and clean out my mailbox. I don't have any other reason for going outside. The freezer is pretty full, and there's still some wine in the cellar."

"What about your company? I know they've had plenty of problems during the past few years and I would think that they probably need their new leader at the tiller almost every moment to guide them out of their troubled waters."

I hesitated. The words were tough to say. "Bill, two days after the funeral I wrote to my best friend on Millennium's board and tendered my resignation, stating that the company certainly deserved more, far more, than I felt I was able to offer them, since it had become a terrible struggle for me just to get out of bed in the morning. It didn't even hurt to write that letter, which gave me a good idea of my state of mind. I had truly buried all my hopes and dreams with Rick and Sally. A couple of weeks have now passed, and I still feel the same way."

"That's a rough, tough board of directors who sit around Millennium's oval table. Six years ago, John, I used up a lot of sweat and tears putting together their pension plan. I've got thirty years of experience in insurance and pension plans, but they made me earn every cent of my commission, and then some. So what kind of response did you get to your letter?"

"One I never expected. They would not accept my resignation. Gave me a four-month leave of absence, with pay, and suggested that I meet with them sometime soon after Labor Day. In my letter I had suggested the names of two vice presidents, both recruited by me, either of which I believed would do well as my successor. The board did name one of them acting president and chief executive officer for four months."

"So ... you'll be back on the job in September?"

I said nothing.

"John?"

What could I tell him? That I never expected to serve another day as Millennium's president? That I didn't even want to *live* another day ... and as soon as he departed, I was going to finish what he had interrupted and kill myself?

"John? John, I'm so sorry. It's much too early for you to begin thinking about going back to work. How inconsiderate of me even to ask. I just came by to offer you my love and my sympathy and to find out if there was anything I could do to make your load a little lighter. Like the old days, remember?"

I patted his knee and mumbled, "Thanks."

Bill rose to his feet, frowning and looking down at me. "I also came for another reason. I need a favor, a favor that no one I know can handle better than you."

"Just ask."

"My station wagon is parked in your driveway. Will you please come for a ride with me?"

"What?"

"A ride. I'd like to take you for a short ride. Won't even leave town, and I promise to have you back here in thirty minutes. I swear!"

Thirty minutes. Such a tiny morsel of time. Time. The world's most precious commodity and increasing in value every day. Franklin had called it the stuff from which life is made, and here was my oldest friend asking me now for *just* thirty minutes, with no idea that if he had come pounding on my window thirty minutes later, he would have found my dead body.

I shook my head. "Sorry, old friend, but I don't think I'd make much of a riding companion, even for that short a time. The last automobile I rode in was a long black Cadillac behind a hearse."

"Humor me, John. You don't have to be a good riding companion. Don't say a damn word if you like. Just come with me, please. Please."

I went.

Neither of us spoke until we had reached Main Street, but when we passed the common and bandstand, Bill said, "They tell me this old town gave you quite a coming-home celebration." Immediately he made a wry face, pounded on his steering wheel and said angrily, "I'm sorry, John!"

I didn't reply. Bill turned right after passing the Baptist church, drove over a small covered bridge and by the time we had passed the old town cemetery, with its leaning thin headstones of slate, I knew where he was taking me. Within minutes we had pulled into a paved parking lot whose far side was guarded by a chain-link fence at least twelve feet tall, on which hung a long blue-and-gold wooden sign proclaiming, in Old English lettering, that we were at BOLAND LITTLE LEAGUE PARK . . . as if I needed a sign to tell me.

I could feel my heart pounding as I followed Bill through the opening on the right-field side of the park between the end of the wire fencing and wooden out-field wall, which curved in a gentle arc from the foul line in right to a deeper point in center to the foul line in left. The number 202, in vivid yellow, was freshly painted at the very edge of the fence in both right and left field, indicating the footage down the foul lines. I remembered hitting a home run over the fence in dead center field, during my last year of Little League, and on the following day my uncle had measured where the drive had cleared the fence—247 feet!

When Bill and I arrived in center field, he stopped, extended his hand to me and said warmly, "John, now you are really home."

I inhaled deeply and turned slowly to my right until I had completed a full 360-degree circle. Then I turned and did the same thing in the opposite direction before I said, almost in a whisper, "Amazing, truly amazing. The park looks exactly as it did thirty years ago! Lots of fresh paint, new wood, neat fencing and a much better parking lot, but it's still our old field! Look, Billy, they still have those small billboard-type ads plastered along the outfield fence in right and center . . . and some of those companies were advertising back when we were playing. And then in left field the wall is just painted green—no ads—exactly like the left-field wall in Boston's Fenway Park that we've always called the 'Green Monster.' "

I pointed up at the scoreboard high above our heads in center field and actually smiled. "Remember how our dads had to climb that ladder alongside the scoreboard platform and post the score, inning by inning? The parents would draw for that duty before the game, and the person whose name was drawn, the 'loser' he was called, was given the numbers on wooden squares, and he would climb that ladder after each inning and hang the proper number of runs scored."

"They're still doing it, John."

I walked slowly toward the infield until I was standing

at my old position, shortstop. Bill stepped back on the grass to the left of where second base would be and we stared at each other. Suddenly and impulsively I slapped my hands together, crouched as if to field a hard-hit ground ball, swept it up in my hands and tossed the invisible ball to Bill, who had moved over and was standing on "second base." He reached up as if to take my throw, turned and threw toward where first base would be. Double play! I applauded.

Arm in arm we walked slowly toward the pitcher's mound. "Look at the grandstands," I said with a sigh. "They haven't changed them a bit! Twenty or so rows high, from behind third base all around the wire backstop behind home plate to just behind first base. Wow!"

Bill nodded. "Seating capacity hasn't changed. Those grandstands hold slightly under a thousand fans. Not bad for a town of only five thousand. Let's go have a seat," he said, pointing to the dugout behind third base.

"Now those are different," I said. "We just had benches, but these are real concrete dugouts, sunk into the ground with steps up to the playing field and a roof overhead. Big-league stuff!"

We stepped down into the dugout and sat on the wide green bench. "The field is in great shape," I said. "This place must get a lot of tender loving care."

"Yes, they're just about ready for the season's start in three weeks. Tryouts are this Saturday morning. The field is ready—but I'm afraid the league isn't."

"What's that mean?"

"Well, with the exception of one year in the past

twenty, we've always been able to come up with enough kids to fill our four-team league with at least twelve players on each squad, and it looks like we'll have enough personnel again this year, just barely."

"So what's the problem?"

"John, my two boys are now in college, so it has been many years since they were involved in Little League. I can't say the same for their father. As you remember, it is tough for many of the players' dads to offer their services as coach or manager because they have jobs that would make it difficult for them to be at most practice sessions, whereas I pretty much make my own hours. So each year I continue to offer my services as coach, and if any of the four team managers can use me, well, I'm his for the season."

"Bill, I think that's great. With your knowledge of the program and experience dealing with these kids I'm certain you're a great asset to any team."

"I hope so," he said. "Anyway several months ago Tom Langley, whose boy was the league's all-star catcher last year, had been selected by the league president and board members to be one of the four managers this year, and he asked me to assist as coach. I agreed of course. Then my angina acted up, and I was pretty sure I'd be out of it this year, if not forever. But when I heard about your ... your trouble, I had to come home in case I could help in any way, and now there's another reason for staying. The league needs me. It seems that Langley was promoted by his company, a month ago, and has already put his house up for sale and moved to Atlanta.

So, one of our teams needs a manager, and there's not much time."

We had been friends for many years. I was almost positive I could sense what was coming. Bill leaned close to me and said, "John, remember I told you that I needed a favor?"

I couldn't look at him. "I thought you just wanted to take me for a ride."

Bill chuckled. "Well, I do in a way. A twelve-game ride. The league officers were a little bit intimidated by your position and success and were hesitant to contact you, especially in light of your great loss, so I offered to explore with you the possibility of your managing a Little League team this year."

"Old friend," I said sadly, "I can't even manage my own breakfast, much less deal with a dozen hyperactive kids straining to break loose from parental authority. I could never do it."

"John, we're all convinced you would make a fine Little League manager. With your background you are familiar with the program and its goals, would be a wonderful teacher and role model and your players would certainly learn plenty from your baseball savvy as well as how to handle victory, defeat, and how to treat your teammates and your opponents. I remember a lot about you, my friend. I know the kids would love you."

"But that love has to flow both ways, Bill, and I'm afraid all of mine is now buried in Maplewood Cemetery."

"I'll help you, John. I'm a damn good coach. And now

that Millennium has given you the summer off, this would be a great way to fill your time for the next couple of months. Might be the best kind of therapy for you, old friend."

I shook my head. "Sorry," I muttered, "I just can't do it."

Bill stood, walked slowly up the dugout steps and headed toward home plate. Suddenly he paused, turned toward me and said, "John ... our last year of Little League together. Remember it? We went undefeated. League champions. Do you happen to recall our team's name?"

"Of course I do. We were the Angels."

Bill nodded. "Well, that happens to be the team that doesn't have a manager this year!"

I closed my eyes for I don't know how long. Then I heard myself asking, "Did you say tryouts were on Saturday morning?"

Bill leaned toward me and said softly, "Saturday at nine. Please consider it, John. I'll drop by around eight-thirty in case you've changed your mind, okay?"

"What day is today?"

"Thursday."

I was several steps behind Bill as we walked slowly on the thick green grass toward the right-field opening and parking lot. Suddenly I saw Bill stumble, quickly regain his balance and reach down. When he turned, he was holding the most bruised, battered and weathered baseball I had ever seen. He placed the ball in my hand and turned away without saying a word.

I V

couldn't bring myself to go inside, after Bill dropped me off at my front door, so I circled around to the rear of the house and walked across the lawn toward the meadow. Dense clusters of tiger lilies in full bloom formed their own aimless and natural maze all the way back to the tree line, and already a dozen or so tall wild blueberry bushes were covered with white blossoms. I stepped closer to one of the bushes and rubbed the palm of my hand gently against the frail flowers. Sally and Rick and I had walked this same path before we had even moved in, and I still remember how excited Sally had become when I showed her the blueberry plants. She had waved both arms high in the air, extended outward to include every nearby bush, and shouted, "You two guys pick them when they're ripe and I promise to bake all the pies and muffins you can eat!"

After gently snapping off a tiny branch of buds and placing it in my shirt pocket, I walked hesitantly down a small slope to the oval pond and sat on the same flat granite boulder, at water's edge, that the three of us had shared that day. We had been told by the realtor that there were both perch and bass in the water, and I had promised Rick that soon after we moved in, he would have his own fishing rod and I would teach him how to use it. I never got the chance.

When I finally returned to the house, I entered through a side door of the attached two-car garage and tapped the overhead light switch. Since I hadn't driven my Lincoln in more than three weeks, I walked around it slowly, checking to be certain that none of the tires had gone soft. The other parking stall, of course, was now empty. Except for two tiny brown oil spots on the cement floor, there was no sign that a car had ever parked there. Along the left wall, nearest the hallway entry to the kitchen, was Rick's red twenty-inch still-scratch-free Huffy "Street Rocker" bicycle, his seventh-birthday present.

In the kitchen I made myself a cup of instant coffee to wash down what had become almost a daily diet: saltine crackers and peanut butter. As I sat at the antique pine harvest table that Sally had insisted on buying, with its matching six chairs, after she had learned that it had been made before George Washington took his first oath of office, I found myself staring at that unique and decorative piece of needlework called a sampler that was facing me on the kitchen wall. More memories.

Some were of my beloved mother, sitting in her wicker rocker after the day's work was done, humming softly as she cross-stitched rows of alphabets, flowers, country landscapes, fruit, and even entire poems on face-towel-size squares of tea-dyed linen, using threads of every color imaginable. Her patience, when handling the tiniest of details, as well as her talent, had won scores of ribbons at county fairs throughout New Hampshire despite some very tough competition.

The sampler in our kitchen, consisting of twelve rows of different-style letters of the alphabet, both upper and lower case, had been my mother's wedding gift to Sally and me and it had hung in every kitchen we had ever occupied throughout our married life. "Some people hang old horseshoes in their home for good luck," Sally had once told my mother, "but in our house it's the precious sampler you gave us." In none of our many kitchens, through the years, had it looked as much at home as it did in this country setting. At the bottom of the framed piece, framed but with no glass—"like they did it in the old days," I remember my mother saying—was her name and date when the work had been completed, *Elizabeth Margaret Harding, August 1954.* I had been all of four years old.

Sitting in that very still kitchen, sipping coffee and making cracker crumbs, I was staring almost hypnotically at the busy sampler I had lived with for so many years of my life when I suddenly remembered how my mother had always dealt with death, even the loss of my father. Mom was very religious, and whenever there was a death in Boland, of either a stranger or a friend, she would make it a point to attend the wake, whether it was at a funeral home or at the person's house. When I was very young, she would often take me along rather than leave me in our neighbor's care. Now, sitting in my kitchen with her sampler before me, it was easy to remember how she went about comforting those in mourning. I'm pretty certain that her powerful words of consolation never changed throughout the years, and recently I caught myself using them to accompany my sympathy at a friend's loss.

My mother, after embracing the grieving spouse or child or parent, would say, very gently, "You must cry no more. Wipe away your tears. Just remember that where your Robert is now, he wouldn't change places with any of us!"

I leaned forward and buried my head in my arms. *John,* I could almost hear my mother's soft voice again, *you must cry no more. Wipe away your tears. Just remember, please, that where your Sally and Rick are now, they wouldn't change places with any of us!*

On Friday morning I was awakened by the guttural roar of power mowers. Bobby Compton and his Homestead Landscaping crew were doing their weekly thing. Instead of pulling the pillow over my head, as I had done in the past few weeks, I rolled out of bed, showered, shaved, put on fresh blue jeans and a clean sport shirt and went outside to greet Bobby. When he saw me, he put down his weed trimmer and hurried toward me, extending his hand and saying, "I'm so sorry, Mr. Harding."

I nodded. "Thanks, Bob."

"We've been mowing here each Friday, even though I didn't have any luck trying to contact you. Was that okay?"

"Of course. I'm glad I've got you. The place looks great!"

"Is there anything special you'd like done?"

"No, just keep doing what you're doing."

"Mr. Harding, I ran into Mrs. Kelley at the village store yesterday. She's awful worried about you. Said she's come by here several times and also tried to phone you often but had no luck."

Rose Kelley had been hired by Sally to be our one-day-a-week cleaning lady. Within only a few weeks we had grown to love her, had virtually adopted her into our family. Rick had even begun calling her Nana.

"Thanks, Bob. I'll get in touch with her. You guys have a good day."

"You, too, sir."

I had orange juice, coffee, and two dry bagels before calling Rose.

"Mr. Harding, oh, dear God, it's so good to hear your voice again!"

"It's good to hear yours, too. I miss you and I know I need you. Please forgive me for not calling you before this. . . ."

"Oh, I understand, sir."

"Anyway, the place is getting messy and dusty. I haven't done much around here since . . . since . . ."

"I know, and I'm so sorry. How about today? Can I come now, or would it inconvenience you?"

"Now is fine . . . or come whenever you like. Just knock hard on the front door, Rose. There's something wrong with the doorbell."

She was at the front door in less than twenty minutes. After a long hug and a few tears, she straightened her green bandanna and headed for the downstairs broom closet. Although Rose was over sixty and couldn't have weighed much more than a hundred pounds, she was incredibly strong and she proved it again by the way she muscled our powerful vacuum cleaner through every room in the house. Before dark, with only a short pause to eat a small lunch she had brought, as always, in a paper bag, the place was looking immaculate. When the old girl came into my studio, to say good night, I jumped up, went over to her and kissed her cheek.

"Next week?" she asked. "Thursday as usual?"

I held out my hand. In it was a duplicate house key that Sally and I, only days before the accident, had discussed giving her. "Thursday is fine. And now you've got your own key so that whenever I'm not here you can still come in and take care of business, okay?"

She nodded and her eyes grew moist. Then she bit her lower lip several times, inhaled deeply and said, "Mr. Harding, as I was going around cleaning, there were . . . ah . . . there were lots of Sally's things, here and there, you know. I didn't know how to ask you what you wanted done with them, so I just kind of left everything where it was."

"That's okay. I'll do some picking up, although I'm afraid that even after everything of hers is put away, she will still be in every room."

Now there were tears running down Rose's cheeks. "And I didn't know what to do in the child's room either, so I just made the bed, put some toys in the toy box and dusted."

"Thanks, Rose. See you next week."

I returned to my desk and sat, chin in the palms of both hands. What was I doing? Maintaining the grounds? For what? Dusting and vacuuming the house? Rick's toys being picked up? Why? What difference did it make? Damn! Damn! I jerked open the lower-right-hand desk drawer and stared at the ugly loaded gun. Same old questions exploding in my head. What was there to live for? Who was there to live for? Who? On my desk was the aged brown baseball, its cover cut and scuffed, that Bill had stumbled over and handed me as we were leaving the baseball park. I picked it up and held it against my cheek. *Oh, God, please help me!*

V

On Saturday morning I had already walked down the driveway and was leaning on my mailbox, waiting, when Bill pulled up in his old Buick. He looked both surprised and pleased at seeing me but said nothing as we rode along, for at least five minutes. Then, still staring straight ahead, he shook his head several times and said, "I'm very proud of you, old buddy."

"Well, I think it would be wise if you withhold judgment for now. I'm not sure I know what I'm doing or whether I'll be able to see this thing through. The odds are great, Bill, that I'm probably going to let you down and run away from this commitment, and sooner rather than later. You've got to understand and be ready if I can't hack it."

Bill reached down and handed me a Masonite clipboard that had been next to him on the car seat. "I typed up a list of all the player applicants last night so that you can make notes while you're evaluating the various kids in the tryout. That red number before each name will be on a piece of heavy paper pinned to the back of each boy's shirt, which should make it easier for the coaches and managers who are judging talent to identify the kids and jot down their opinions and ratings for each of them. We're trying it this year for the first time. Should make the Monday-night player draft a lot easier and certainly speed it up."

"And what's this other number, the one after each name?" I asked.

"That's the boy's age. Just to refresh your memory, the magic date is August first. Kids must be nine before that date and not thirteen until after that date in order to play—ages nine to twelve, as it has always been. By sheer chance we happen to have no nine-year-old applicants this year, but there's a good mix of tens, elevens, and twelves."

"Some of these names are underlined. What's that all about?"

Bill grinned. "Well, I figure the other three managers have a little jump on you since they've lived here for years and know most of the kids. Also, they all managed last year, so they've got a pretty good reading on the available talent. The names I underlined are the twelve kids I think are the most outstanding athletes. The three names with double underlines are the best three pitchers, at least as I remember their performances from last year. But this is your team," he said, patting my knee, "and your flock of Angels will all have been selected by you."

"However, you will share your expert opinion with me, correct?"

"If you ask for it," he said, smiling.

As soon as we stepped out of the car, in the Little League parking lot, I could hear them—the children—shouting, laughing, calling out to their fellow players, accompanied by an almost rhythmic thump of baseballs being caught in leather gloves. It was still early, but obviously most of the playing candidates were already on the field doing whatever they believed was necessary to attract some manager or coach's attention.

It had been one thing for me to walk out on a quiet and empty field the other afternoon with Bill, but this was much tougher. I don't know what I expected, but the kids didn't look much different or sound much different or even act much different from the way my young buddies had, almost thirty years ago, when this field had been the most hallowed ground in the entire world to me. I closed my eyes, listening to the sounds, and tried to remember my very first Little League try-out. I was just a few days past my ninth birthday, nervous and frightened, and my dad had driven me here, to this same field, in his pickup. Just before I turned away from him, in the parking lot, and ran out on the diamond for the first time, he extended his hand, smiled and said, "Break a leg, son!" I knew what he meant because that strange phrase had come up at dinner one night, and mother had patiently explained to both of us that those words were how show people always wish each other good luck before a performance. Break a leg!

"John?"

I opened my eyes. Bill was several yards away and frowning. "Are you okay?"

I shrugged my shoulders and nodded. He pointed toward the first-base dugout. "Let's go meet the league officials while we've got time."

Boland Little League's president, Stewart Rand, was already an acquaintance, since he was an officer in the local savings bank and we had met on that morning when Sally and I had opened our checking and savings accounts. He rose from the dugout bench when he saw us approaching and extended his hand toward me before Bill could say anything. "Mr. Harding, I can't tell you how pleased we are to have you with us. We all welcome you, with open arms, as well as extend to you our deepest sympathy. Thank you for your willingness to share your time, your effort and your considerable baseball knowledge with our youngsters. I'm certain they will be better players and citizens because of your counsel, leadership and example. Forgive the speech"—he grinned—"but I truly mean every word of it. You are a very special man, and I'm glad we've got you."

I mumbled my thanks. Then Bill introduced me to Nancy McLaren, the league's secretary-treasurer, followed by three members of the board, the other three managers and their coaches as well as several parents, all of whose names I forgot soon after the introductions.

At last, in response to a single shriek from a whistle that had been hanging around President Rand's neck, the players ceased their throwing and running and noisily took seats in the lower rows of stands behind the dugout. Parents, who had been scattered throughout the grandstand, now began moving to positions in upper rows, behind the boys, in order to hear, while the league president waited patiently for everyone to get settled, waving and nodding constantly to people calling out his name. When the chattering in the stands finally subsided, he raised his right hand and said loudly, "Good morning, parents and players and friends of Boland Little League. My name is Stewart Rand. As this year's league president, I welcome you to the opening session of what will be our forty-fourth year as a chartered Little League. That means that, through the years, we have proudly sent several thousand of Boland's youth out into the world, imbued, we hope, with qualities of teamwork, fair play, courage, persistence and discipline that have made them better adults and better citizens."

Stewart Rand paused, smiled and then said, "We have a good deal to accomplish in the next couple of hours or so and we shall try, with the generous assistance of our managers and coaches and several parents, to give every player an opportunity to show what he can do at bat, on the bases and in the field. And, while all that energy is being expended on our historic field, our four team managers, upon which so much responsibility rests for the next two months, will also be moving around the field from group to group, observing and judging and making notes so that on Monday night, at the draft, they will be able to assemble four good competitive teams for our exciting twelve-game pennant race."

Bill and I had been standing, with the other managers and coaches, behind Rand. Bill turned and said softly, "I'll get together with you later." Then he moved slowly toward the league president just as Rand was saying, "And now I'm going to turn this morning over to an old friend of mine and many of you, Bill West, who will co-ordinate the various activities."

The tryouts lasted until well past noon. Each player was allowed half a dozen swings at the plate, hitting pitches tossed by one of the coaches who had the unique ability to throw ball after ball in the strike zone. During the long hitting session at least six boys took their turns behind the plate, catching. Four were allowed on the infield at one time, while the batting was taking place, and they were told to go to their position of choice and to field anything that was hit toward them. While all this was happening, another coach and parent were stationed in deep right field, behind the foul line, hitting towering fly balls to a second group of youngsters. After perhaps forty-five minutes the outfield group came in to the dugout, batted, and then assumed positions in the infield, while those who had been batting and playing the infield moved to the outfield. As all that organized chaos was transpiring on the field, another, smaller group had gathered behind the first-base dugout, where there was a pitching rubber and plate. They threw to catcher candidates for more than half an hour while all four managers watched intently. Often, at the request of a manager or coach, another young athlete would be called in from the field and asked to pitch for several minutes with the emphasis on control—how many pitches were near or over the plate.

Not until just before noon did I get a chance to confer with Bill. Swinging a bat as he would a golf club, he came over to me and said, "Well, skipper, what do you think?"

I handed him my clipboard, saying, "Pretty tough to really evaluate all these kids in just a couple of hours, but I did take a crack at grading them numerically, ten down to one, plus jotting down a few comments to help me remember some of them on Monday night at the draft."

He studied my board for several minutes, nodded and handed it back. "John, you don't need any advice from me. What did you do about pitchers?"

I handed him the clipboard again and said, "I marked the best pitching prospect P-one, the next P-two and so on, but of course everything will depend on when we get to draft. Whoever drafts first will no doubt go for my P-one, he's that much of a standout."

Bill nodded. "You're absolutely right. Todd Stevenson was not only the best darn pitcher in the league, last year at age eleven, he also batted over four hundred, hit five or six home runs and played first base when he wasn't pitching. He was very special. Didn't you say you were rating the kids from ten down to one?"

"Yes."

"But there's nothing next to this kid's name," he said, handing the clipboard back to me.

"I know. Number thirty-six. God love him, he's so tiny and slow and uncoordinated that ... I just didn't know what to put down. But he never quit, never stopped running and never seemed to get down on himself after missing pitch after pitch at the plate. Do you know him?"

Bill leaned closer to the clipboard and squinted. " 'Timothy Noble.' No. Must be a new family in town."

I pointed toward the group in center field still taking turns catching fly balls from a coach's bat. "Third from the left, Bill. In those baggy pants. See him? Your list shows he's an eleven-year-old, but he's got to be the smallest player on the field."

As we were talking, the little guy moved away from the other players, who turned and watched, nudging each other and snickering. Obviously the next fly ball to be hit was his to catch. Leaning forward, he flexed his knees and pounded his right fist into his glove again and again.

"My God!" I said half aloud.

"What's the matter ... what am I missing?" asked Bill as he glanced around the outfield.

"Nothing ... nothing."

How could I tell him that Timothy Noble, not much bigger than my beloved seven-year-old, looked just like Rick from a distance as he crouched and leaned forward on his toes, waiting. The coach swung his bat and arched a long fly ball toward Timothy, who circled helplessly beneath the ball, waving both his arms toward the sky. As the ball descended, he first turned to his left, then to his right and began to run, but somehow his feet got tangled and he fell headfirst onto the grass while the nearby group of players moved close to each other, almost in a huddle, with several holding their hands over their mouths as they fought back giggles.

A few minutes later the youngster failed, once again, to get under a fly ball hit to him, and it landed several feet away. He raced toward it, picked it up and threw it back toward the batter. The ball landed no more than forty feet from where Timothy had been standing and the other players turned away, smiling. Timothy momentarily brushed the back of his right hand against both eyes.

"He sure is tiny," said Bill. "How old did you say he was, according to our list?"

"Eleven."

"Well," sighed Bill, "he's certainly going to be a challenge for the manager and team who end up with him. Probably will be one of the last kids drafted. Still, according to the rules, he's going to have to be played in each game, for a minimum of six defensive outs, and he'll have to go to bat at least once per game. I'm afraid that any balls hit in his direction, wherever he'll be playing, even for two innings, could prove very costly."

We looked up to see Timothy Noble on the move again. This time he overran a tall, lazy fly ball that dropped behind him. As he tried to stop suddenly, his tattered sneakers slipped on the grass and he fell, tumbling over onto his side. Still, he jumped up quickly, wiped the grass clippings from his T-shirt, yanked down firmly on the bill of his old baseball cap, retrieved the baseball, ran in several steps toward the coach who had hit it and threw the ball with so much effort that he fell over backward. The ball, after completing a small airborne arc, rolled along the grass until it finally came to rest at the batter's feet. Those who were watching cheered loudly while they mockingly applauded. Timothy Noble turned, faced his hecklers and tipped his cap.

"Look at him, Bill," I said softly. "The kid is smiling."

VI

❧

*S*aturday afternoon, or what remained of it after tryouts had ended, was spent behind my house, on the deck, reading, rereading and highlighting in glowing yellow many paragraphs in the *Little League Baseball Official Regulations and Playing Rules.*

Soon after I had started my second pass through the sixty-four pages of rules, I found myself reading a small piece, written by the Chairman of Little League Baseball, in which he briefly presented leadership qualities by which any local manager could be evaluated. Many of them sounded familiar to me until I realized that the traits necessary for good leadership, including many I had worked hard to acquire and live by in my own business career, were universal and as old as time and that they would certainly work in successfully guiding a Little League team as well as they worked in any board room: compassion, understanding, setting a good example, cooperation, teamwork, reaching toward mutual goals, encouragement, praise, and always striving to improve. Each of the activities listed were indeed vital to a good leader, in any enterprise, but somehow I had never expected to find such wise and valuable advice in a baseball book of rules.

Reviewing the hundreds of "shalls" and "shall nots" among the pages of playing rules brought back memories of my own Little League experiences, but they faded quickly from my mind. The Chairman's brief but powerful message was forcing me to take a long look at myself, and what a sorry image it was. John Harding, widower, no immediate family, currently on "employment leave," despondent, aimless, potential suicide. Should that John Harding be leading a Little League team? Never! What I was about to become involved in was foolish and irresponsible, and those great kids I saw trying so hard this morning certainly deserved far better than me. How could I encourage them? How much sympathy and compassion did I have to dispense? How could I make any attempt to understand their home life while I was struggling to deal with the grim fact that I no longer had one of my own? And how could I possibly set a good example for them, fill them with enthusiasm and desire, teach them how to think positively—and never quit, never quit(!)—when I, their manager, their leader, was ready to quit the greatest game of all—life—and really didn't care if I even lived to see another sunrise? This situation was truly my fault.

In my depressed condition I had bought Bill West's great sales pitch because he had always been such a special friend, but it just wasn't fair to those young and impressionable boys at an age when they already had enough problems. Not fair! However, I still had time to bail out. Then I remembered how Sally had always acted as my manager whenever I had been confronted with situations in the corporate world that I didn't think I could handle and didn't want to deal with. She would cup my face in the palms of her hands, look straight into my eyes and say, "Hon, I've never, ever seen anything or anyone beat you and I positively have never seen you give up. You can handle this problem just like you've handled every other. Just be yourself and you'll come out fine."

I shoved the rule book into my back pocket and slid open the glass door leading to the living room. After walking slowly across the room, I paused a yard or so away from the fireplace, leaned forward and stretched out my arms until both hands were tightly gripping the wooden mantel. I stared down at the hearth. To my right was a small copper pail filled with kindling wood and an old folded newspaper, and next to it was a brass log holder piled high with split maple logs. Sally had insisted that we really couldn't claim to be official residents of our new home until we christened it with our first fire in the fireplace, so she had quickly located a local source for wood and had it delivered and stacked along one wall of the garage. I recall, so vividly, that chilly evening back in March when I had come home late after a very rough day at Millennium, found a roaring fire in the fireplace and a proud wife anxiously waiting for my reaction. With her tiny hands clasped tightly together, as if she were pleading for mercy, and blue eyes opened wide, she had asked anxiously, "Well, how did I do?"

I remember saying, "You've just bought yourself another chore, lady, especially on Christmas morning."

Rick was already in bed, so the two of us had sat on the sofa, very close to each other, holding hands and touching heads, staring contentedly into the gold-and-crimson flames. . . .

I pushed myself back from the mantel, turned and stared at the empty sofa, feeling so lost and alone. Then I pulled back the black-mesh screens covering the fireplace opening, reached inside and opened the chimney damper and within ten minutes I had a fire blazing. After stacking logs on the fire, as high as the top of the andirons, I slid the mesh screens closed and slumped down on the sofa—only now it was early June and I had no Sally to hug. . . .

For municipal budgetary reasons it had almost become general practice throughout New Hampshire in the past twenty years or so to have consolidated school districts, each composed of students from clusters of small adjoining towns. But the very independent town of Boland had remained autonomous, with its own school system. And so, when Bill West drove into the parking lot at Boland High School on Monday evening, it was another trip backward in time. Twilight was falling, but I could see that the red-bricked, single-story exterior looked almost exactly as it did when I had graduated in 1967. Inside we walked down a polished-tile corridor. The walls, which held several cork bulletin boards filled with notices and student artwork, were painted in familiar beige. I paused outside one of the doors, on which the gold numeral four was printed high on the frosted glass. Bill turned, staring at me until I pointed toward the door and explained, "My homeroom. Senior year. Suppose it's okay to peek inside?"

"Don't see why not."

The door was locked.

We continued down the hall and entered Room 8, where the draft was scheduled to be held. Stewart Rand and Nancy McLaren were both standing near the teacher's desk. Behind them, on the large blackboard, were printed the names of every player who had participated in the Saturday-morning tryouts.

"Good evening, gentlemen," Stewart called out. "Please take seats anywhere, and we'll be ready to commence in just a few minutes. Thank you."

First I followed Bill as he went up aisles, shaking hands with his old friends. Although I had met them all at the tryouts, I was introduced to the other team managers and coaches once again. We found two empty seats near the front and tried to force ourselves behind two small desks.

"I guess we've both grown a little since the late sixties," Bill said, chuckling as he tapped his stomach.

Stewart Rand began striking the side of a drinking glass with a ruler, and all conversation and laughter gradually subsided.

"Okay, everyone, before we begin this year's draft, let me quickly review a few points. The fact that a player was on one particular team last year does not automatically place him on that same team this year. There is no team-player carryover. All players will be drafted by you to the team on which they will compete this season. Is that understood?"

Rand glanced around the room until several heads nodded.

"I've been asked why there are no girls involved in our league. They are, of course, entitled to participate as well as the boys, and of course they have in many past years. However, the girls' softball program in this town, for all age groups, has become so popular that apparently the young women seem to have elected to compete in their own league, so this year, for the first in several, our teams will be composed totally of males.

"Now . . . before we begin our drafting process, I ask a small favor. Would each of the managers kindly stand, introduce himself, name his team and tell us in a few short sentences what he hopes to accomplish this year."

Rand waited patiently until a well-muscled man wearing a New York Yankee T-shirt rose and said, "My name is Sid Marx, and I understand I shall be managing the Yankees with the help of this fine gentleman, sitting to my right, Don Pope. This will be my third year as manager, and I'm honored to have these kids under my care.

My fervent hope and prayer is that Don and I can teach them some of the many values they will need to live a life filled with success—and more important, peace and contentment."

A tall, gray-haired man in a well-tailored business suit stood and said, "My name is Walter Hutchinson, and I'll be handling the Cubs along with Coach Alan LaMare, who could not attend this evening because of business. This is my second year in the league, and although I look forward to improving my last-place finish of last year, I realize that there are other goals in our program than just winning baseball games. I know only too well, from my own life's experiences, that participating in Little League can be a wonderful training ground in helping to shape the character of our young men."

"My name is Anthony Piso," said a short, stocky man who had been sitting in front of me. "I'm probably the only grandfather managing a Little League club in all of New Hampshire, but this year the Pirates will be handled by me and this man here, Jerry White. I've been managing for six years, and for the first three of those years my grandson, who now lives in Arizona, was on the team. He's the one who got me into this. During my years as manager I've won two championships and look forward to building another good team, which will probably be my last, since my doctor doesn't think that getting excited as I do, during the games, is doing very much for my cardiac condition. I hope to walk out, at the end of this season, with my head held high, but even more important, I want to make some contribu-

tion, once more, toward helping a dozen kids take another step in the right direction on this tough road
called life."

There was a slight rippling of applause as Piso took
his seat, grinning. "Just like a politician," someone behind me said loudly, and everyone turned toward the
old boy smiling. Puzzled, I glanced at Bill.

"Tony is Boland's town treasurer, John. Has been for
more than twenty years, I guess. Now it's your turn,
buddy."

I rose, inhaled deeply and said, "My name is John
Harding, and I'll be managing the Angels, with a lot of
help from my friend, Bill West. I'm extremely honored
to be a part of Boland Little League again, after so many
years, and I truly appreciate the opportunity you have
all given me to teach and work with these fine boys. I
fully realize that I have much to learn about this important position and I hope that I can count on all of you
for advice when I seek it. The precious lives that have
been entrusted to us deserve every opportunity to develop to their fullest potential. I'm honored to be part of
this program."

Stewart Rand, smiling slightly, nodded in my direction and said, "Gentlemen, thank you. And now . . . the
big moment! The rules governing our player-selection
process are quite simple. You four managers will each
draw a number from this old baseball cap of mine. The
manager drawing number one will select first, number
two, second, and on through each of the four managers.
Then, in order to keep things fair and to equalize the

talent among the four teams, we will select in reverse order in the second round. The manager who drafted
fourth in the first round will draft first, the manager
who drafted third will select second and so on. Since
there are forty-eight eligible players, there will be a total of twelve rounds. As soon as you have drafted a
player, Nancy will bring you an information card with
his address, parents' names and phone number. You will
want to phone the young man to inform him as to
which club he'll be playing for and also give him the
time and place of your first practice.

"One final point of order. Sid and Walter have sons
who will be playing in our league this year. They are
both excellent players, and so, in keeping with our local
rules and custom, they will be considered as having
been drafted by their father's team as part of the second
round of the draft. I believe this is fair to all four teams.
However, if anyone objects, let's hear from him now."

There were no objections.

"Okay, gentlemen. There are four folded slips in this
cap. Will each of you kindly come up here, remove a
slip from the cap and hand it to Nancy."

I was last in line, so Stewart reached in for me,
handed my slip to Nancy and I returned to my seat. She
opened all four slips, made notations on her legal pad
and handed the pad to Stewart.

"Gentlemen, here is the order in which you will draft
to commence things. Beginner's luck! John Harding of
the Angels will draft first; Sid Marx of the Yankees, second; Walter Hutchinson of the Cubs, third; and . . .

sorry, Tony, Anthony Piso, Pirates, will select fourth. Are you prepared to draft your first Angel, John?"

"I am. The Angels take Todd Stevenson."

Sounds of moaning and groaning filled the classroom. Sid Marx turned and grinned in my direction, saying, "Todd will pitch his game a week and win them all, so you've already got six victories in the sack. Win just three out of the other six and you've got yourself a championship."

"Sid . . . Sid . . . if only it were that easy," Bill said with a sigh.

"I know. Only kidding, John."

The entire draft took almost two hours. Very often coaches and managers checked and rechecked their notes, and on several occasions they went out into the hallway to confer in private. It was obvious, from the beginning, that these men were really familiar with the available talent. Fortunately I had Bill West and I leaned on his judgment heavily as we went through round after round of selections.

Finally we were in the last round of the draft and there were only four candidates who had not been chosen. Heavy lines had been drawn through all other names on the blackboard as well as on every manager's and coach's list of players. Bill leaned toward me, reached out toward my list and pointed to one of the names through which there was still no line drawn, Timothy Noble. I glanced over at him. He was shaking his head from side to side. The eleven players we had selected so far seemed like a well-balanced group. I was pleased with our team, at least on paper. Now, just one more selection.

It didn't take long. Piso, Hutchinson and Marx all had their pick ahead of us, and after they had made their choices, there was only one name remaining on the blackboard without a white chalk line running through it.

Timothy Noble became my last . . . my twelfth Angel.

VII

For the next three weeks each of the four teams in our league practiced two afternoons a week, usually from four P.M. to six P.M. One weekly practice session for each team, according to the schedule Nancy had distributed after the Monday-night draft, was at Boland Little League Park, and the other was on a smaller baseball diamond behind the park, owned and maintained by the town, adjacent to the playground, which boasted swings, sandboxes, seesaws and even several horseshoe courts for the older folks.

Following our weeks of practice, the official season would commence. Each team was scheduled to play twelve games, two games a week for six weeks, with four games played against each of the other three teams. All games would be played at Little League Park on Monday, Tuesday, Wednesday and Thursday evenings, commencing at five P.M. Should a game be rained out, it would be rescheduled for Friday evening or Saturday morning. Actually two postponed games could be played on Saturday if necessary. After each team had completed its twelve-game schedule, the two with the best won-lost record would play one game for the league championship.

On our way home, after the draft, Bill West offered to phone the players we had selected to inform them that our first practice would be at Little League Park on the following Tuesday afternoon at four, but I told him that if I was going to manage the team, then I believed it was my duty to get on the phone. He looked surprised, then pleased, then grinned and nodded his head approvingly.

Shortly after seven on Tuesday evening I settled down at my desk in the den to notify twelve young men that they were now Angels. Shuffling the individual player cards that Nancy had handed us following each of our selections, and reading the names on our roster, one after another, made me think that we had not only drafted for Little League but also for a little League of Nations: Todd Stevenson, John Kimball, Anthony Zullo, Paul Taylor, Charles Barrio, Justin Nurnberg, Robert Murphy, Ben Rogers, Chris Lang, Jeff Gaston, Dick Andros and Timothy Noble.

Bill West had left me with a gentle warning when he dropped me off after the Monday draft. Most of the kids were familiar with him, the other three managers and every coach, but I was a stranger in town, an unknown factor that might cause our players some unease and uncertainty, at least at first. It was a wise observation, and I thanked him. Before making any phone calls I scribbled some notes on a legal pad, outlining a simple procedure for me to follow once I was on the phone as well as some key words to use. Dialing each player's phone number, I would ask for him first after identifying myself, no matter who answered the phone. I would then welcome the boy to the Angels, tell him he had been selected because he was a fine ball player and that our first practice was scheduled for next Tuesday at four. I would then ask if the boy had a ride to the park and someone to pick him up at six after each practice. Many, I discovered, got around Boland quite well on their bicycles. I had forgotten how independent country kids always are. After chatting with the player I would ask to speak with his father, introduce myself to the gentleman, tell him that I was proud to have his son on my team and ask him to call me, at home, anytime, if there was anything he wished to discuss concerning his son during the season. I would close by mentioning that I was looking forward to meeting every parent at one of our practices or games soon and that I would certainly be grateful for their support. If the father was not at home when I phoned, I would have a similar conversation with the boy's mother. My final phone call was to little Timothy Noble.

"Timothy Noble?"

"Yes."

"Timothy, this is John Harding, Little League manager of the Angels. I'm calling to tell you that you will be playing for the Angels this year."

"All right!!!"

"First practice is next Tuesday at four o'clock at Little League Park. Can you make it okay?"

"Yes, sir! I'll be there!"

"Will you be able to get a ride to the field and then home? Practice will end at six o'clock—always."

"I have a bike, sir. I'll be there. Mr. Harding, could you please tell me some of the other guys on the team?"

"Sure. Todd Stevenson, Paul Taylor, John Kimball, Anthony Zullo—do you know any of those fellows?"

"I'll be playing with them? Wow! They're all great. We'll have a good team, a super team!"

"And I'm counting on you to do your part, Timothy. Now, is your dad around? I'd like to talk with him if I may."

The little guy's lilting voice immediately fell several octaves, and he replied swiftly, in a flat, husky monotone with no hint of emotion, "My dad lives in California."

Caught off guard, I hesitated. How to reply? Finally I said lamely, "Oh . . . well, could I speak with your mother?"

"She's not home from work yet."

I glanced at my watch. Exactly seven-forty.

"Oh. Ah . . . okay, Timothy, we'll see you on Tuesday afternoon."

"Yes, sir. And . . . Mr. Harding, sir?"

"Yes?"

"Thank you very much for picking me. I'll try hard to do good for you."

I hung up slowly. My heart was suddenly pounding. While talking to Timothy I had turned my head to the left. Among a cluster of framed family photographs, hanging on the wall nearest me, was a color enlargement of my Rick wearing a slightly oversize baseball cap, staring intently at the camera while he crouched menacingly with his aluminum baseball bat cocked behind his right shoulder. I rose, walked slowly from the room out onto the deck, sank limply into the chaise rocker and remained there, staring off into the distant woods until long after darkness fell.

It was a tortuously long seven days, waiting for the team's first scheduled practice session. I worked very hard at trying to fill every waking moment with some sort of activity, either of body or mind or both, so that I didn't stumble and fall into that always nearby pool of despair. I would force myself out of bed at seven each morning and after breakfast went off for a long hike through the woods behind the house. Then I would take my red practice shag bag of golf balls and my short irons and stroke shot after shot from one golf pin to the other in our backyard. After darkness I would jog for perhaps an hour, return, shower, and put on my pajamas and robe. Then I would sit at the kitchen table, despite the far more comfortable chairs in other rooms, and try to read. During the years of struggling up corporate ladders, I had acquired a large collection of some of the world's best self-help and inspirational books to assist in my climb, classics such as Allen's *As a Man Thinketh*, Hill's *Think and Grow Rich*, Peale's *The Power of Positive Thinking*, Stone's *Success Through a Positive Mental Attitude*, and Danforth's *I Dare You*. Now I spent countless hours each evening, searching through these and scores of other books, hoping to find special words of wisdom or consolation that might help me to deal with the pain of my loss. In an old leather-bound nineteenth-century anthology of wise sayings I finally discovered some precious words of solace from Benjamin Franklin and Antiphanes, a Greek dramatist from the fourth century before Christ.

At the funeral of a close associate Franklin had told mourners, "We are spirits. Our friend, as well as all of us, were invited abroad on a party of pleasure which is to last forever. His chair was ready first and so he has gone before us. We could not all conveniently start together and why should you and I be grieved at this, since we are soon to follow and know where to find him."

Amazingly, more than two thousand years earlier, Anthiphanes had written, "Be not grieved above the measure for thy deceased loved ones. They are not dead, but have only finished the journey which it is necessary for every one of us to take. We ourselves must go to that great place of reception in which they are all of them assembled and, in this general rendezvous of mankind, live together in another state of being."

Once again I remembered my mother's similar advice to those mourning the loss of a loved one. Accepting that advice, whoever was giving it, required a giant leap of faith. God, how I wanted to believe their words!

During that long week of waiting I renewed two other common activities of life, answering a telephone and driving an automobile. Don't know what made me pick up the phone on Wednesday morning to hear Bill's surprised voice on the other end. After that he called every morning just to check on me. As to the driving, I went nowhere in particular, just backed my car out of the garage one afternoon and drove around the back roads of New Hampshire for a couple of hours. In spite of all my efforts, however, I still went into my den at least once each day, pulled open the bottom drawer of my desk and stared down at the gun. Once I picked it up and held it cupped in my hands for several minutes. The deadly thing felt very cold, almost as if it had been packed in ice.

Even though I pulled into Boland Little League's parking lot early, for our first practice session, Bill West was already there ahead of me, removing two large canvas bags from his car's trunk, one containing catchers' equipment and boxes of baseballs and the other filled with batting helmets and bats.

"Let me give you a hand," I yelled, coming up behind Bill and lifting one of the bags. Together we walked through the fence opening and turned toward the nearest dugout, behind first base, as the players who had arrived early came running toward us while, in the parking lot, several car doors slammed as mothers dropped off their hopeful athletes.

Bill passed out some baseballs, suggesting that the boys pair off and begin warming up. Some were dressed in blue jeans and T-shirts, others wore last year's now-tight baseball pants. Some had baseball shoes, others wore sneakers, high and low. Soon we had two rows of six players, tossing balls back and forth, a few very serious and obviously nervous, while others were laughing and loose. Bill and I casually walked behind first one row of six players and then the other, introducing ourselves to every boy. Each was told, as we shook hands, that I was John Harding and he was Bill West. The word *coach* would be fine for both of us if they didn't want to call us by name, and we said that there was no need for 'sir' or 'Mister.' Also, as we chatted with each new Angel, we asked him what position he liked to play and if he had participated in Little League last year. Gradually we could sense that all players were beginning to relax. The smiles multiplied.

It was amazing to me how much we managed to accomplish during that first practice. Bill West sent groups out to the shortstop and second-base positions and hit several balls to each player, who had to field the ball and then throw it to first, where there were two candidates for that position. I stood in short right field and observed how players moved and reacted to Bill's hits. Two of them, Anthony Zullo and Paul Taylor, fielded flawlessly and threw to first with good accuracy. The Taylor kid, in a tight T-shirt, had a great upper body, which I was sure had taken a good deal of time and effort to develop.

We repeated the same procedure with our outfield candidates, hitting several ground balls and fly balls to each of them. We also had them throwing the balls they fielded back to our only catcher candidate, John Kimball, looking for strong arms that might be converted into another pitcher or two. Two players, Charles Barrio and Justin Nurnberg, looked very fast and competent and could throw.

Eventually Bill hit three fly balls to little Timothy Noble. Two he failed to get under and the third caromed off his glove and rolled far behind him. The ground ball hit to him went right through his open legs.

At our second practice session, on Thursday, we commenced by putting a tentative team on the field based on our observations from the first practice, with Bill hitting both ground and fly balls to each position while I walked around and offered suggestions on the best way to catch a fly ball, how to position oneself to best handle a ground ball and, most important, how to throw a baseball properly. I was very impressed by our catcher, short, muscular John Kimball, who had two years of Little League under his belt and a cannon for an arm. Any baseball team, amateur or professional, without a good catcher plays under a terrible handicap. We were very fortunate to have Kimball.

During our third practice, at the other ball field behind Little League Park, we concentrated on hitting. I threw batting practice so long that my arm began to tremble as Bill made notes on his clipboard pad. Both of us stopped play often to correct batting stances, strides and swings. There was no doubt that Todd Stevenson, our star pitcher, was also our best batter. He hit several of my pitches out of the park, and his smooth left-handed swing was a joy to watch. Our catcher, Kimball, whom the players had already nicknamed Tank, also hit well, as did Paul Taylor and a tall boy, Justin Nurnberg, who looked like he might be our first-baseman during the games that Todd pitched. Then, when someone else pitched, we would put Todd at first base so that we'd still have his potent bat in the lineup, and we'd probably move Justin to the outfield, although he was a much better fielder at first.

Eight players looked like certain starters, even after only the third practice session—Stevenson, Kimball, Zullo, Taylor, Nurnberg, Barrio, Murphy and a great fielder but weak hitter, Ben Rogers, who was a natural at shortstop. Three other players, Chris Lang, Jeff Gaston and Dick Andros, showed potential and were certain to get better with practice and experience. And then there was Timothy Noble, who had been the last to bat. I had tried to pitch the slowest possible balls to the little guy, but his stance was so awkward and his swing so choppy that I felt embarrassed for him as his new teammates giggled each time he swung at the ball and missed, until I turned and stared at them and it became very quiet.

I glanced at my wristwatch. We had sent word home to all parents, via their sons, that we would not run any practice beyond six P.M. so that dinners could be planned accordingly. It was now five minutes to the hour. I clapped my hands together several times and yelled, "Okay, guys, that's it for today. See you all Thursday, at four, on Little League Field!"

Most of the boys immediately raced to the parking lot and their bikes or their waiting car ride home. Timothy, however, was still standing at the plate, looking very concerned, swinging the bat he was holding back and forth. I glanced toward the dugout where Bill was loading bats and helmets into one of the canvas bags. There was no one else on the diamond when I walked slowly toward the plate and said, "Timothy, can we talk for a minute?"

"Sure," he replied, his voice quivering slightly.

"Timothy," I said, "I believe that if you work very hard and put in some extra time and practice, you could become a good ballplayer. The more we practice something, the better we get at it. It's kind of hard to work very long with one player when all the guys are here, but I think I can help you with your hitting and fielding if you let me. Tell me, would you be willing to spend an extra half hour after practice, just with me, concentrating on a few basics? I know that with a little work we can really improve that swing of yours, and maybe I can give you a few tips that will help you handle fly balls and grounders a lot easier. We have three more practices before the games begin. What do you say?"

Knees bent, I had been crouched down so that I was talking to him at eye level, and for a brief moment as he took a half step forward I thought the little guy was going to leap into my arms.

"I'd like that very much," he said, biting on his lower lip.

"Would your mother mind? Might mess up a couple of her evenings. Late dinners. What do you think?"

"That would be okay. She works at Edd's Supermarket in Concord and doesn't get home until around eight o'clock. She works from eleven to seven, Monday through Saturday."

I didn't understand why, but I found myself fighting to hold back tears.

"Okay, Timothy, we'll do it. How about tonight? Want to start right now?"

His brown eyes opened wide, and for the first time I noticed the faint band of freckles that ran from one cheek to the other, across the bridge of his nose. He nodded vigorously.

"And Timothy, we don't have to say anything to the other kids. We wouldn't want them to think I'm playing any favorites here, okay?"

He nodded again.

I turned toward the dugout. Bill West, although he was too far away to hear us, was watching and smiling. Finally, and before I could say anything, he said, "John, I'll leave the bag with the baseballs and bats right here. You two have fun. I don't think you'll need me. I will see you both on Thursday."

"Good night, Bill."

VIII

The Angels, as a team, made far more progress than either Bill or I had dared expect of them during our final three practice sessions in the ten days leading up to our first game. In all sports, I'm certain, the majority of coaches spend most of their time concentrating on the mechanics of playing well. Our challenge was to teach the fundamentals of fielding, hitting and running, as well as the rules of the game, to active, energetic youngsters who are at an age when concentration on any one subject for more than five minutes is usually a major achievement.

During each of the practices we devoted the first hour to hitting and running the bases and the second hour to fielding and reviewing the playing rules. Beginning with the fourth practice, I asked Todd Stevenson, Paul Taylor, Charles Barrio, and Justin Nurnberg to come to the park thirty minutes before the others and to commence strengthening their pitching arms by throwing to either Bill or myself so that we could further evaluate their potential. Todd, of course, was without question our ace pitcher, while the other three would compete for spots in our pitching rotation. According to Bill West, both Taylor and Barrio had pitched at least one winning game during their previous season of play, and Nurnberg threw so hard that we couldn't ignore him.

For the batting sessions Bill and I split the pitching time, tossing soft throws across the plate while the other, standing off to the right of the batter, would make countless suggestions and corrections, ranging from having the youth try another and usually lighter bat to positioning him nearer or farther from the plate or showing him how to stride smoothly through the swing instead of lunging at the ball. Bill asked Paul Taylor, our muscular third-baseman and now pitching prospect, to try spreading his feet until they were as far apart as his shoulders were wide. With this more comfortable and solid batting stance, an enthusiastic and now-excited Paul began hitting long fly balls over the fence in center and left field. Ben Rogers, our shortstop and smooth fielder, seemed to chop down on every pitch, either missing the ball completely or driving it into the dirt. It amazed us that someone who fielded with such grace looked so awkward at the plate. We worked on leveling this quiet and unsmiling young man's shoulders and hips just before he swung. Soon his bat was making much better contact. After hitting three consecutive long fly balls to center and left he caught one of my pitches flush, and I watched the ball sail down the left field line until it cleared the fence by at least ten feet. Dour Ben was actually smiling when he jogged past me to the outfield.

To accomplish as much as possible in the limited time available, we also tried to combine base running with our fielding drills, stressing again and again how important it was for our base runners to know exactly where that baseball was at all times, since they should run the bases with as much aggressiveness as they could. We also worked on the fundamentals of bunting, and timed all our players with a stopwatch, again and again, not only from home plate to first base but also from first to second. Little Tony Zullo and Todd Stevenson were easily the fastest, while Tank Kimball, our catcher, took so long to get from first to second that Bob Murphy, our team comedian, said he was much too slow to be called Tank.

The final thirty minutes of practice were devoted to reviewing the playing rules. We realized that there was no possible way we could cover every rule and subclause in the entire sixty-four pages of *Little League Baseball Official Regulations and Playing Rules*, but we concentrated on as many as possible, covering situations that we believed might arise again and again, such as why one should guard against getting hit by a ground ball as he is running the bases, when he can and cannot leave a base once he has reached it safely, and especially what his demeanor should be toward spectators, opposing players and umpires, and the penalty for acting otherwise.

Of course I now had an additional activity to help occupy my mind and a little more of my time: the practice sessions, one on one, with Timothy Noble after our regular team practice. On the afternoon following our third practice session, when he had both surprised and touched me by quickly accepting my offer of some additional coaching, the two of us first sat alone in the quiet dugout and had a long chat.

"So tell me, Timothy, have you been playing baseball most of your life?"

Sitting on the bench, quite close to me, his short legs didn't reach the ground. He stared down at his dangling feet for several minutes before shaking his head slowly and replying, "No. My dad was in the army and we lived near Berlin in Germany for a long time, and the kids there all played soccer. I liked soccer, but I wasn't very good. Couldn't run fast enough. Then we came back to the United States last year, to live here in Boland, but pretty soon Dad went away from us and he never came back and my mother was sad. Then she got a divorce."

Again, as on the telephone, Timothy was speaking in a flat, emotionless monotone, sounding almost like a toy robot. *My father is gone. There, I've told you. Now let's not talk about that anymore.*

"So you've only been playing baseball for a year or so?"

He nodded vigorously, brushed back loose strands of

blond hair that had escaped his old baseball cap and smiled. Then he threw out his tiny chest, kicked forward with his two legs, clenched both fists, raised them above his head and shouted loudly, "But day by day, in every way, I'm getting better and better!"

"What did you say?" I gasped.

"Day by day in every way I'm getting better and better!"

I couldn't believe my ears. Impossible! I inhaled several times, trying to calm myself, unable to grasp how the little guy had just managed to repeat the very same powerful words that had once played such a vital role in *my* life. One of the greatest and most positive influences during my early years of corporate-ladder climbing had been a tiny book written by a turn-of-the-century French healer, Emil Coué, titled *Self-Mastery Through Conscious Autosuggestion.* Coué believed that he could help others rid themselves of nearly every affliction, from serious physical problems to negative mental attitudes, if they learned to make positive and healthy suggestions to themselves again and again. Coué eventually became a great cult figure, and his lectures attracted thousands, both in England and in the United States back in the early days of this century. Vast audiences listened and believed that it was possible to rid themselves of scores of life's illnesses and wounds by merely repeating their positive goals and desires again and again. The Frenchman's work was best exemplified by his most famous self-affirmation, "Day by day in every way I am getting better and better!" Millions repeated those words, aloud and to themselves, time after time, day after day, and so did I after I discovered them in a thin black-leather volume in a secondhand bookstore. That powerful self-affirmation worked for me. Primarily because I *believed* the words. They kept me optimistic and hopeful. My mental attitude, despite any temporary setbacks, always remained positive. I *knew* things would be better tomorrow. I *was* somebody! I *would* succeed! It was almost impossible to think negative thoughts while announcing to the world and to myself that "day by day in every way I am getting better and better!"

Coué and his process of conscious autosuggestion faded from popularity long before the great depression, and he had his share of critics, as do all pioneers in the fields of medicine and psychology. But from my own experiences I knew that positive thoughts programmed into my subconscious mind through self-affirmations, either repeated aloud or to myself, produced positive results, and my favorite was "Day by day in every way I am getting better and better!"

"Timothy," I asked after I finally closed my mouth and took another deep breath, "where did you learn that saying?"

He frowned and glanced at me suspiciously. Finally he said, "From Doc Messenger. He's nice. He's very old, but he always takes care of me and my mother when we get sick. When I saw him the last time, he played catch with me and told me if I kept saying those words, lots of times each day, I would get better at whatever I was doing, even playing baseball. Doc Messenger is nice. He comes to see me practice, sometimes."

"Oh, was he here today?"

"Uh-huh. He was sitting behind first base all by himself. Today he was wearing a cowboy hat. He waved at me. He has a white beard."

"Has he taught you any other sayings?"

Timothy nodded, threw out his small chest and said, "Never . . . never . . . never . . . never . . . never . . . never give up!"

I knew that one too. Winston Churchill's commencement address to a graduating class at Oxford. Eight words . . . eight very powerful words. Then the great man turned away from his audience and walked slowly back to his seat.

"Do you believe those words, Timothy, that one should never give up?"

He nodded. "I never give up."

We spent our first practice working on Timothy's hitting. I would stand next to him, also holding a bat, and ask him to imitate my stance and swing. Worked better than I had hoped. After ten minutes or so I began pitching to him while correcting any variances in either his stance or his cut at the ball. Before long Timothy was taking short strides into my pitches with a level swing and even following through while maintaining his balance. He only made contact a few times, but I could see that his confidence was gradually building, and he seemed to be enjoying our routine. We even spent time practicing bunting, and although he had difficulty pivoting and keeping his arms relaxed, I finally had him crouching and bending his knees until he dropped several fine bunts down the third-base line.

That evening, at home, I phoned Bill.

"You okay?" he asked quickly, unable to hide his concern.

"For the moment."

"How did it go with your little Angel?"

"Fine. Fine. He's getting better and better. . . ."

"What?"

"Nothing. Bill, I was wondering, are you familiar with a Doc Messenger in this town?"

"Everybody is, John. Old Doc Messenger has practiced here for a long time. He was a big man on the staff at Johns Hopkins and came here to Boland after he retired—to grow a few tomatoes and hit some golf balls, he told everyone. Then Boland's only doctor suddenly moved to Seattle, and this township had no one to take care of them, so the old man decided to come out of retirement and he's been Boland's savior ever since. Even makes house calls for sick kids and old folks. Why are you asking about him? Something wrong, John? Need a doctor?"

"No, no. Timothy was telling me about the good doctor. Seems like he's quite a special man. According to Timothy I guess he's even come to a couple of our practices."

"I thought that was him sitting high up, back of first base, wearing that old hat of his. Never gave it another thought when we got busy. Didn't figure him to be spending time at a Little League practice."

"Timothy said he came to see him."

"Well, since he probably helped deliver most of our team into this world, as well as the rest of the league, I imagine he's keeping his eye on all of them. Quite a guy! Must be almost ninety, but he can still hit a golf ball a long way, believe me."

During our final two practice sessions Timothy and I worked on his fielding and base running. On fly balls I began by merely tossing them up into the air, coaching him to hold his hands over his head and catch the ball with both. After he had caught perhaps ten tossed balls in a row, I grabbed a bat, sent him out to shallow center field and began hitting gentle pop-ups. It seemed to take him far too much time to see the ball in flight before he moved toward it. I wondered if his eyesight was at fault, but he said he had been checked at school in May and they had told him that his vision was normal. Could it be his reflexes, perhaps? I didn't know. Also, his running was terribly slow, whether he was chasing after a fly ball or going from base to base, and the expression on his tiny face, when he ran, was always one of great effort. I finally asked him, "Timothy, does it hurt you to run?"

"No," he gasped. "I just keep trying to make my legs go faster, but they don't. They will, though, you wait. They will. I'll never give up . . . never! I'll be faster!"

Following our final preseason practice each player received his official Angel uniform, gray with the letter *A* in large dark-blue script on the left side of the shirt. The caps and socks were also in dark blue, and as Bill handed a box to each player, he said he hoped and prayed that he had measured everyone correctly.

I was loading bats and balls into the canvas bags when I sensed that Timothy was standing close by.

"Yes, Timothy?"

"Mr. Harding, thank you very much for all your help. My mother said to tell you thank you for her too. I know I'm a better player now." He grinned and then said, "Day by day . . . day by day. . . ."

I smiled and extended my hand. "Good luck, all season. You're going to do fine, trust me."

He nodded enthusiastically. I wanted to pick him up and hug him as I had always hugged Rick.

"Good night, Mr. Harding."

"God bless, Timothy. Don't forget. First game next Tuesday at five against the Yankees. Be here no later than four-fifteen."

I stood and watched until bike and rider turned the corner and were out of sight. Then I returned to the dugout and sat until long after darkness had fallen, praying to God for the strength to hold on. . . .

IX

J hadn't felt so nervous since that memorable day, not very long ago, when I had stood to address the board of directors of Millennium Unlimited for the first time.

All the pregame activities had been completed and the opening-day ceremonies were now drawing to a close as everyone in Boland Little League Park rose to the strains of our national anthem from the loudspeaker system affixed to the top of the tall wire backstop.

It had been almost thirty years since I had played my last Little League game, but the routine prior to the game had not changed even a little in all that time. The first-, second-, and third-base canvas bags had already been anchored down at their proper spots on the diamond by the time Bill and I arrived at the park and unloaded our equipment. Since we were the designated home team for this opening game, our dugout was the one behind third base.

Bill broke out our ball bag, and our lads started throwing on the sidelines. Sid Marx, the Yankee manager, waved in our direction and then came across the diamond, shook hands, and we wished each other good luck. Each team took infield practice, Yankees first. When it was our turn, I hit three easy grounders to Paul Taylor at third, Ben Rogers at shortstop, Tony Zullo at second and Justin Nurnberg at first. Although they were all obviously tense, our infield handled all my batted balls flawlessly. Behind our dugout Todd Stevenson had already started his warm-up throws to Tank, while behind the Yankee dugout a very smooth left-hander named Glenn Gerston, who had impressed me at the league tryouts almost as much as Todd, was throwing hard. This opening game was probably going to be a low-scoring pitchers' battle.

Two umpires finally made their entrance through the opening in the fence that separated the field from the parking lot. Both were wearing light-blue shirts, open at the neck, dark-blue pants and baseball caps. One was carrying a chest protector and mask. When they arrived at home plate, they beckoned to Sid and me to join them, and after more hand shaking all around the umpire with the chest protector said that there was only one special ground rule for our field. Any batted ball that landed in the outfield in fair territory and then bounced over the five-foot-high wooden fence that bordered the outfield, whether on the first bounce or the tenth, would be considered a double.

George McCord, a popular Boston morning-radio personality on WBZ and WBZA Radio for more than thirty years, before retiring to Boland, had been the League's public-address announcer for several years, the "best nonpaying gig I ever had," he kept telling everyone. I had heard nothing but praise for the old boy's ability to make every name in the lineup sound as if Ted Williams were coming to bat in the last half of the ninth with two out and the score tied.

After our meeting with the umpires, George's husky voice was heard, from his position at a bench and heavy oak table behind the home plate wire backstop, introducing Stewart Rand, who dramatically announced that the forty-fourth season of Boland Little League was about to commence. He instructed the Angel players, coach and manager to form a single file along the third-base foul line, from home plate, and the Yankees to do the same along the first-base line. Then he asked our Todd Stevenson if he would please walk out to the pitcher's mound and lead both teams in the Little League Pledge.

Todd turned to me in surprise, but when I patted him on the shoulder, he trotted out to mid-field, removed his cap with his left hand and placed his right hand over his heart. His voice quivered slightly as he began, but soon he was almost completely drowned out by twenty-three other eager and youthful voices.

"I trust in God. I love my country and will respect its laws. I will play fair and strive to win, but win or lose, I will always do my best."

All our players immediately turned, as they had been instructed to do, and ran back to the dugout as soon as the pledge had been completed. When they were all seated, I sat on the top dugout step facing them and said, "Well, guys, we've been working hard for several weeks to get to today. Just keep your mind on the game and keep doing the things you've been doing in practice and I know you will do well. We've got a good team. Now, let's go out there and start proving to everyone that we're the best team in the league!"

"We'll never give up!" little Timothy suddenly blurted out.

"Yeah," responded Todd. "We'll never give up!"

"Never give up, never give up, never give up!" the entire team was shouting when the plate umpire nodded toward us and pointed to the field.

"Okay, men," Bill barked, "let's go get them!"

As soon as the Angels had all taken their positions, accompanied by applause, cheers and whistles from the stands, the national anthem commenced, and every player on both teams faced the flagpole in deep center field, standing at attention with his cap clutched tightly to his chest until the music stopped.

Todd threw eight or nine final warm-up pitches to Tank before the home-plate umpire stepped in front of the plate and turned his back toward Todd as he leaned down to brush off the plate. Then he returned to his position behind Tank, put on his mask, adjusted his chest protector and yelled, "Play ball!"

I had decided to say nothing to Todd before he went out to the mound. No motivational pep talk. He had thrown well in warm-up and he looked to me as if he had things under control. Anything I said to him might do more harm than good if it affected his concentration. I went down into the dugout and sat next to Bill and our three nonstarters, Chris Lang, Dick Andros and Timothy.

"Bill," I said, "I just can't believe the size of this crowd. It's only five o'clock on a Tuesday afternoon, but this place is almost packed solid. Close to a thousand fans for a Little League game in a town of only five thousand or so people? Seems impossible."

"Not here in Boland, John. If you checked the stands, you'd find a lot of parents who care but also a large number of retired people who don't want to or can't afford to move to warmer climates. These games have become an important part of their lives. They will all select a favorite team as the season begins and cheer for that team all season. Gives a lot of them something to do, a place to visit and maybe a reason to wake up and get out of bed in the morning, something a lot of them need very much."

A reason to want to wake up and get out of bed in the morning? One never misses it until that desire isn't there anymore. Oh, how I knew! I turned toward Bill, but he was staring out toward home plate, and his face showed no emotion. I patted him on the knee and said nothing.

Timothy Noble had moved to the top dugout step. His shrill voice suddenly resounded above the crowd noise, "Come on, guys, you can do it! Never give up, never give up . . . !"

Todd had a little trouble with the fresh sand around the pitching rubber and he walked the Yankee lead-off batter before settling down and retiring the next three batters in order on two grounders and a strikeout. As our team came in from the field, I called to Chris Lang, sitting on the bench, and asked if he would mind being our first-base coach. Without saying a word he jumped up and trotted across the diamond toward first. I would give the batters and base runners all the signals from my third-base coaching position, signals as to whether they should bunt, take the next pitch and also whether or not they should attempt a steal if they were on base. Bill West had agreed to monitor things from the dugout as well as keep our scorebook to be certain that every boy played the allotted number of innings.

Tony Zullo walked to lead off our half of the inning, and I decided to test the Yankee catcher's throwing arm immediately. The league rules declare that base runners shall not leave their bases until the ball has been delivered and has reached the batter, and when the first pitch to our second batter, Justin Nurnberg, was called a strike, I immediately touched my left elbow with my right hand, signaling that Tony was to break for second base as soon as the next pitch crossed the plate. Standing at the plate, Justin also picked up my sign and swung well above the next pitch in order to distract the catcher as Tony broke for second. Zap! The ball was waiting for him when he hook-slid into the bag, and we knew in a hurry that the Yankees had an excellent catcher as well as a smooth pitcher. Then, as so often happens when a runner is thrown out stealing, Justin stroked a clean single to right field, but Paul Taylor, batting third, struck out on three pitches, bringing up Todd. The big guy hit the first pitch high to left field, and the scrambling young man out there, with more luck than skill it seemed, made a sensational catch over his right shoulder just before he ran into the outfield fence. Fortunately he was only shaken up, but he did hang on to the baseball and the crowd gave him a well-deserved standing ovation as he ran across the field into the Yankee dugout.

Both teams were scoreless in the second inning, although Bob Murphy stroked a beautiful double down the right field foul line before Jeff Gaston popped up to end our threat.

"Never give up, never give up!" Timothy Noble had become our self-appointed cheerleader. Stationing himself at the far end of the dugout, he repeated his favorite words again and again as he jumped up and down, both fists clenched tightly, while his teammates urged him on, often asking for more as they joined in: "Never give up, never give up!"

Both teams were scoreless after the third inning, and

as our guys were preparing to take the field to start the fourth inning, I substituted with my other three Angels, as we had planned. Chris Lang took over for Tony Zullo at second base, Dick Andros for Bob Murphy in left field and Timothy Noble for Jeff Gaston in right. Our subs would play the fourth and fifth innings. That way we would have all our regulars back in the lineup for the final inning.

Todd seemed to be getting stronger with every inning. He struck out all three Yankees who faced him in the fourth inning, and the Yankee ace, Gerston, almost matched him pitch for pitch, striking out two of our guys and allowing the third to hit a short pop fly to first base. Four innings of our six-inning game were now in the books. Still no blood. More and more it was beginning to look like one of those contests that is often decided by a single break.

The first Yankee batter in the fifth hit a hard drive to third that Paul Taylor did a great job of knocking down, but before he could pick up the ball and throw it to first, the batter had crossed the bag safely. The next batter struck out on three pitches, but the boy who followed hit a hard smash to deep shortstop. Ben Rogers dove for the ball, speared it in his mitt, leaped to his feet and fired the ball to Justin at first. Sensational! The batter was out by inches, but the runner who had been on first slid safely into second without a challenge. Now the Yankees had a man in scoring position, with two out, and their pitcher, Gerston, who batted as he threw, left-handed, was coming to the plate.

Bill leaned toward me and said softly, "If you know any prayers, John, now is the time to say them. I remember from last year that this kid pulls every ball he hits down the right-field line and he hits them hard!"

I immediately jumped up, called "time" and walked toward the third-base foul line, waving Timothy farther back toward the fence and closer to the line in right field. Finally I held up both hands, palms facing outward, and he stopped moving. Bill nodded as I climbed back down into the dugout.

Todd's first pitch to his mound opponent was a sizzling fast ball. Gerston wasn't waiting. He swung and smashed a high fly ball to deep right field.

"Oh, God," I heard Bill saying.

Timothy ran back several steps, staring up at the evening sky. Finally he turned and raised both his hands high above his head as the ball reached the top of its long arc and started its fall.

"He's right under it," yelled Bill as we both rose to our feet. "Come on, kid, grab that apple!"

The ball's descent was agonizingly slow. Timothy hesitated and then took another step backward, his glove held high, but the ball seemed to bounce off the tip of the glove's frayed fingers and landed on the grass behind him, rolling all the way to the fence. By the time Tim had retrieved the ball, one run had scored and Gerston was standing on third base, waving both hands high in the air while the crowd continued their applause. Todd struck out the next batter, but the Yankees now had a one-run lead.

As Timothy came down the dugout steps, I could see that his face was streaked with tears. I started to speak, but he just looked up at me, shook his head and hurried to the far end of the dugout. None of his teammates spoke to him or went near him, although there were a few angry glances. Sometimes kids can be so damn cruel. Bill rose and faced the bench after they had all taken their seats. He waved his scorebook and said, "Okay, men, our first three batters are Lang, Andros and Noble. We've got six more outs and we're only down by one. This is anybody's ball game, so let's get them!"

Chris Lang hit a feeble pop fly to the pitcher, Dick Andros went down swinging and then Timothy Noble approached the plate. His teammates, who had been shouting words of encouragement to both Chris and Dick, were suddenly silent. Standing in the batters' box, Timothy tugged at his pants, which seemed at least a size too large for his tiny frame. He dug in with his sneakers, assumed a slight crouch and waited. Gerston's first pitch was an inside fastball that almost hit Timothy, but he never backed away. He lunged at the next two curves and then stepped out of the batter's box, taking a deep breath and rubbing his hands in the dirt. Then he took another deep breath and stepped to the plate, his bat cocked as we had practiced. Gerston took a long and deliberate windup before he reared back and fired his fastball. Timothy's swing was smooth, but the ball made a loud sound as it plunked into the catcher's mitt. He walked slowly back to the dugout, placed his bat carefully along the row of bats and returned to the far corner of the dugout, biting his lip.

The Yankees were retired in order again, in the sixth and final inning, but the Angels couldn't do much better. Tony Zullo did hit a line-drive single directly over second base, but Justin and Paul popped up to the infield, and Todd's long fly ball was the game's final out.

Todd had pitched a masterpiece, allowing one scratch hit, and yet he had only a loss to show for his magnificent effort.

"Okay, guys," Bill yelled as our team gathered in front of the dugout. "Let's get in a single file and congratulate the Yankees for a good game. Then will you all please come back here and have seats in the dugout for a couple of minutes. I know your folks are waiting, so we won't be very long."

Following the compulsory shaking of hands and "nice game" exchange from players of both sides, the Angels retreated to our dugout. I had never seen them more quiet or subdued as I stood to remind them that there was another game on Thursday and we would do a lot better. However, before I said anything, Todd jumped up, zipped his warm-up jacket, turned and walked down the dugout to where Timothy was sitting, his head in his hands. The dugout was suddenly very still. Todd leaned forward, placing his hands on his tiny teammate's shoulders and said loudly, "Hey, buddy, don't blame yourself. Even big-league superstars make errors. This just wasn't our day, okay? That doesn't mean we gave up. We never give up. Right? Never! You too! Okay?"

Timothy looked up at Todd, his eyes filled with tears. He nodded his head and replied softly, "Okay."

There wasn't much that needed to be said by me after that. "Our next game is with the Cubs, Thursday evening at five, boys. I'd like you all here by four, please. Paul Taylor is our scheduled pitcher. See you all on Thursday."

Driving home I replayed the game in my mind, agonizing along with Timothy as the ball bounced off the fingers of his glove and rolled to the wall. And then, suddenly, I was reliving another game, one I had played during my second year of Little League when I was only ten. I had made two errors, playing second base, and both errors had allowed a run to score. Final score had been a loss for my Angels of old, 3 to 1, because of me. Long after everyone had left the park, I walked out to the grass behind second base, slumped to the ground and bawled my eyes out. I don't remember how long I sat there, but I was too ashamed to go home and tell my dad what had happened. Finally, when it was almost dark, I saw the shadow of an old pickup drive into the parking lot, its headlights diffused by the wire fence. Soon I heard his familiar voice, filled with love and understanding, saying to me, "John, I think it's time to come home."

When I was finally on my feet, I hugged him ferociously, sobbing and crying. All he said was, "It's all right, it's all right. Hell, we all have bad days now and then. Ain't nobody perfect."

Suddenly I hit my brake pedal. I was almost home,

but I pulled over to the side of the road, made a U-turn and headed back to the ballpark. Twilight was giving way to darkness when I parked, walked through the fence opening and headed toward home plate. I could hear children shouting and laughing in the neighboring playground, but our playing field was empty—almost empty. He was sitting in the shadows on the grass in deep right field, his legs folded under him, elbows on knees, head bent forward. I walked slowly toward him and paused when I was about ten feet away.

"Timothy," I called.

His head jerked upward. "Yes?" he said, squinting in my direction.

"Are you okay?"

"Uh-huh."

"Don't you think its about time you headed home?"

He shrugged his shoulders.

"Why are you still here, Timothy?"

"I don't know. I guess I thought that if I just sat out here, where it happened, I'd be able to figure out how I messed up and lost us the game."

"And . . . have you come up with an answer?"

He shook his head, and I heard a muffled sob. Suddenly I had an idea.

"Could I please see your glove?"

He frowned, then reached under his right knee and tossed me an object, the most shredded and nonserviceable baseball glove I had ever seen in my life, its old leather dry, hard and cracked in thousands of places with virtually no padding remaining in its palm or any of the fingers. Also, the webbing between thumb and forefinger was missing and someone had replaced it with strands of clothesline cord.

I flipped it back to him and said, "That thing should be in a baseball museum. It was probably used by Joe DiMaggio when he was a boy."

"No, it wasn't," Tim replied, a smile briefly flickering across his small face.

I leaned down toward him and extended my hand. He took it, and I pulled him to his feet, saying, "Don't you think it's about time you headed home?"

"I guess. . . ." He sighed.

I pointed to his old glove. "And I believe that's your problem—that glove. It's tough to do any job well without good tools."

The little boy stroked the top of the glove softly. He was obviously too embarrassed to tell me what I suspected, that his single-parent mother couldn't afford to buy him a new glove. I tugged at the visor of his new blue team baseball cap with the gold letter *A* and said, "Timothy, there's an almost brand-new Darryl Strawberry glove at home in a closet. It belonged . . . to . . . to . . . my little boy . . . but he didn't get many chances to use it. It's just hanging there now. I'll bring it for you on Thursday."

He stared up at me intensely. "Your little boy is dead, isn't he?"

"Yes . . . yes, he's dead."

"I'm sorry."

I just nodded. "Now, maybe you had better come a

little early on Thursday so that we can play catch for a while and start getting that glove broken in, okay?"

He nodded. "Thank you. I will. I'm sorry I lost the game. I hope the kids don't hate me too much. I feel awful, but I'll try harder, I promise."

"You'll never give up, will you?"

He shook his head and grinned. "Never!"

"Very good. Now, let's get home before it's dark. Do you have a light on that bike of yours?"

He nodded.

"Okay, see you Thursday, early."

"Good night, Mr. Harding."

Just as I was opening the door to my car, Timothy pulled alongside on his bike, the tiny headlight mounted on his handlebars shining brightly in my direction. "Mr. Harding, can I ask you a question?"

"Of course. Shoot."

"How did you know that you would still find me here at the park?"

I wasn't sure what to say to the little guy, but finally I replied, "I don't know, Timothy. I think maybe my dad told me you'd be here."

"Oh."

The bicycle turned, and its light beam began moving slowly out of the parking lot. Before it was out of sight, I heard a small voice shouting, "See you Thursday, Mr. Harding!"

X

ednesday seemed to last for a week. After breakfast I tried all the time-passers I had been using lately. I jogged for perhaps an hour, worked on my pitching wedge in the backyard until I had hit at least two hundred golf balls back and forth, and tried reading, but my mind just kept wandering. I was constantly hearing voices in the other rooms. Sally? Rick? I even turned on the television set, late in the afternoon, but ten minutes with Oprah and then Phil had me diving for the "off" button. I didn't need any more pain.

I went to bed early, soon after the sun had set, and of course awoke before dawn on Thursday. With my eyes still closed and my head buried in my pillow, I reached across to touch Sally as I had done for so many years. Not feeling her soft body, I moved my hand gently and slowly across the width of the smooth, cool pillow before I sat upright in bed and pounded my forehead with the palm of my hand. What are you doing, dummy? Sally isn't lying next to you. Sally is dead. Dead. And so is your baby. So is Rick. Dead. Gone! Never to return!

I finally rose and showered. Didn't feel much like shaving, but then I remembered our game that evening. Couldn't let the parents of our Angels think their kids were being guided by a sloppy bum.

After an omelet, orange juice and coffee, I went into the studio, sat at my desk and stared at the page in our Little League scorebook that Bill had used to record our first game. We had only made three hits off Gerston, singles by Zullo and Nurnberg and a double by Murphy, so there didn't seem to be much I could do to improve the batting order based on game performance. Everyone had fielded amazingly well, except for Timothy's costly error, considering it was our first game. Unless Bill West had any suggestions otherwise, we would go with the same lineup and batting order this evening against the Cubs, except that Paul Taylor would pitch, Justin would move to third base and Todd would play first.

I closed the scorebook, again thinking about that terrible moment in bed when I had tried to touch my lady and there was no one to touch. I tugged at the bottom desk drawer, and it slid open easily. The ugly revolver was still resting on the glossy yellow cover of a NYNEX phone book that contained the listings for Concord residents and several neighboring towns including Boland. I reached inside the drawer but immediately withdrew my hand before making contact with the dark-blue metal.

"Good morning, Mr. Harding."

I nudged the drawer closed with my right shin, acting like any kid who had been caught with his hand in the cookie jar. Some cookie jar!

"Rose. Good morning. I didn't hear you come in, and I guess I forgot it was your day to clean."

The old gal's smile immediately faded. "Is this a bad day, sir? I can come back some other time."

"No, no. Today is fine. It's just me. Too much on my mind, I guess."

Rose Kelley gripped the handle of our vacuum cleaner with both hands and tilted her head sympathetically. "I'm sorry. Is there anything special I can do for you?"

I shook my head.

"Mr. Harding, I hope you won't mind. I went to Maplewood Cemetery yesterday morning and said a few prayers at the grave, for Sally and Rick. It is a lovely spot on that small rise near the stone wall. Have you selected a gravestone for them as yet?"

"No, I haven't."

"Do you go there often, to be near them?"

I stared down at my hands.

"Mr. Harding . . . ?"

I shook my head again. "I haven't been there since the funeral, Rose. I've driven to the cemetery many times, but I've never parked the car and walked along that little path to their graves. I can't . . . I just can't bring myself to get close enough . . . to look down at the grass . . . and . . ."

"Mr. Harding, please forgive me, for I am just an ignorant old cleaning woman, but you must go to the grave. You must. Not for them. For you! I remember my mother, God rest her soul, telling me an old Irish tale that she said had been passed on to her by her grandmother in County Galway. It seems that a young woman in a small village on the coast lost her only son in a fall from a cliff, and in the months that followed his burial she lived a life filled only with constant tears, anguish, heartbreak and mourning. When her dead son's next birthday arrived, she resolved to spend the entire day at his grave, and on the way to the cemetery she stopped to buy some flowers from an old man in the village square. After paying for her cemetery posies she started to leave, but paused to watch the old flower merchant who was carefully picking all the dried leaves and stems from the lower portion of a potted plant that seemed to have no life. 'Why are you wasting your time on that dead thing?' she asked and he replied, 'It is not dead. Oh, some of its leaves have finished with their lives, but see, up here, there is still some green showing in the stalk. I expect that with care and love this plant will live and produce flowers for many more years. Young lady,' he said, 'there are many people like plants. They suffer what is a terrible loss—perhaps a child or a wife or husband—and they allow what has happened to turn them into a shriveled stalk, empty of hope and life.

On the other hand, there are many, don't you know, who will suffer the dried-up parts to just drop off and then they go right on living and breathing and singing and smiling as they keep producing lovely flowers, year after year, just as long as God can use them.' "

"Mr. Harding," Rose continued, sounding more and more like a stern first-grade teacher as she lifted the vacuum cleaner off the rug. "We already have more than enough plants that have perished, back there in the woods. I don't want to see you shrivel up in sadness until you become one of them."

Some time in the afternoon I remembered that I had promised to bring Rick's almost-new baseball glove to Timothy. I went into my son's room, walked directly to the closet without looking left or right and pushed open the sliding doors. The glove was resting on a shelf I had built low enough so that Rick could store some of his more prized possessions at a level he could reach instead of stashing everything under his bed and dresser. Beneath the glove were boxes of Chinese checkers, dominoes, Trivial Pursuit Jr. Edition and Lego. Alongside were brightly colored Ninja Turtles and G.I. Joe action figures mingling with missile launchers, helicopters and Pizza Throwers, all surrounding a towering brown cylinder filled with Tinkertoy parts. Then there were the three cardboard shoe boxes filled with baseball cards. I lifted one off the shelf and held it lovingly in my hand. How many hours had Rick sat at our kitchen table, carefully transferring cards from one indexed box to another as he continued to invest most of his allowance in his collection? I reached in and randomly pulled out a card: "NOLAN RYAN, Texas Rangers." One of Rick's favorite players. Mine too.

Timothy was waiting for me, pacing back and forth in the parking lot, when I arrived at exactly three-thirty as promised. He came racing over to my car, and as I stepped out, I flipped him the glove.

"Oh . . . wow . . . this is cool!" he exclaimed as he slid his tiny left hand into the leather finger slots. Then he pounded his clenched right fist, again and again, into the darker oiled palm of the glove as he flexed the heavy leather webbing that was between thumb and forefinger.

"Want to give it a tryout?" I asked.

"Okay!"

Bill West had all the team supplies and equipment in his car, but I had remembered to bring a baseball and my old glove. The two of us played catch in right field until the other players started to arrive. As Timothy and I strolled back in toward the infield, I asked him, "Does it feel comfortable on your hand?"

"Oh, yes. It's a very good glove, Mr. Harding. Thank you. Thank you. I'll do better now, you wait."

"Day by day . . . , Timothy?"

He grinned and nodded enthusiastically.

After a scoreless first inning our guys jumped on three Cub pitchers for eleven runs, and when I sent in my three substitutes in the fourth inning, the score was already 15 to 1, so I let Chris and Dick and Timothy play the rest of the game without putting the regulars back in for the sixth inning. Final score was an embarrassing 19 to 2, and although we did get fifteen hits, the Cubs helped our cause by committing seven errors. I apologized to their manager, after the game, but Walt Hutchinson was a good sport about it all and said that the way his guys played, they deserved to get clobbered. We had two batting stars. Todd hit two home runs and a double, and Paul Taylor, besides pitching a four-hit game, striking out eight and walking only two, hit a home run and three singles. Timothy came to the plate twice during those final three innings. He struck out both times. No tears, no tantrums, no self-pity, no temperament. Instead by game's end the gutsy kid was hoarse from cheering for his teammates, and apparently they had all forgiven him for his error costing them the first game. "Day by day, in every way, we're getting better and better!" and "Never—never—never—never—never—never give up!" were chanted so frequently and loudly by our team, at Timothy's urging, that the spectators immediately behind our dugout picked up on it, and soon the entire grandstand crowd on our half of the field was repeating those valiant words, over and over, "Never give up!"

On Tuesday evening of the following week our opponents were the Pirates, managed by grandfather Tony Piso, who was also the town of Boland's treasurer. The Pirates had won their first two games, including a 9-to-8 slugfest against Sid Marx's Yankees, who had clipped us in the first game. We knew this was going to be a tough

one, and it was. We won, 2 to 0! Todd Stevenson allowed just one hit, a scratch single between short and
third, and Tank Kimball singled to deep center in the
fourth inning, driving in both Zullo and Nurnberg, who
had walked and been advanced to second and third by
a fine Paul Taylor bunt. We totaled only five hits, all
singles. Timothy did finally make contact with two
pitched balls, both of which he fouled over the backstop behind home plate before striking out, but he
cleanly fielded a Pirate single, which had gone between
first and second, and tossed it to second in time to prevent the runner from advancing. Day by day . . .

After the game I spent at least an hour shaking hands
and talking to our kids' parents. What a great thrill to finally be accepted, but even more important than their
kind words was hearing the unsolicited words of praise
they were repeating that had come from the mouths of
their youngsters about Mr. Harding and Mr. West.

On the following evening, Wednesday, we played Sid
Marx and his Yankees for the second time. Our boys
were out for revenge, and they got it. With Paul Taylor
pitching another fine game, we won, 6 to 4, and this
time our hitting star was Bob Murphy, who had a perfect night with two singles and a double. Two of our
subs managed to get their first hits of the season. Chris
Lang hit a short pop fly to right that dropped in for a
single, and Dick Andros hit a hard line drive shot to
left-center that went for two bases. It was a close and
exciting game. Some of the parents afterward said that
the difference between winning and losing had been our

little cheerleader, who never stopped urging his buddies on. Timothy, now the only player on our team without at least one hit, went down swinging, once again, in his only time at bat, but he hung in there on every pitch and never gave up on himself. As Timothy was running out to his right-field position for the fifth inning, patting his teammates on the back, Bill nodded in his direction and said, "John, that kid's heart must be so big, I'll never understand how the Lord got it inside such a tiny body."

Two weeks of the six-week season were now on the books, and to our great joy and surprise the Angels were leading the league with a 3 and 1 record while the Yankees and Pirates were close behind, at 2 and 2 for each of them. We still had four weeks and eight games to play. Anything could happen.

After that second Yankee game Sid Marx, their manager, and I had a rather long and friendly chat as we leaned against the wire backstop behind home plate. I liked Sid. We covered every possible subject, from the huge growth of the Little League program to how the kids of today compare with those of twenty and thirty years ago in ability and attitude. Sid finally said, "John, it's getting late, and I had better get rolling before Susie starts worrying about me. It was a good game, but we'll get you next time, I promise."

Driving home, I had passed through the old covered bridge and just turned right on Main Street when I saw the little guy, despite near darkness. He was moving along at a steady pace, but he stopped suddenly when I

pulled my car close to the narrow grass edging that separated the sidewalk from the street. I leaned over and
pushed open the car door on the passenger's side.

"Timothy, you're walking home from our game?"

"Uh-huh."

"Why? Where's your bike?"

"The chain broke this morning. My mother took everything to the bike shop in Concord on her way to
work today."

"Hop in and I'll take you home."

"I don't mind walking. And I don't want to bother
you. I'll be okay. Don't worry."

I tried to replace the warmth in my voice with some
authority. "Hop in!"

As soon as he was in the car and the door was closed,
I said, "Now, show me the way." Following Timothy's in-
structions, we continued along Main Street through the
center of town, turned right on Jefferson Avenue and after about two miles of bumpy asphalt we swung left on
Route 67. We continued for about another two miles
before I finally turned to Timothy and asked, "Did you
walk all this distance to the ballpark today?"

Head bowed and clutching his new glove to his
chest, he looked up at me through those long brown
lashes and nodded, hesitatingly, as if he had been
caught in some crime.

"Good Lord, how long did it take you to go from
your house to the field?"

He shrugged his shoulders and sighed. "I don't know.
I left the house around two o'clock, right after I made a

peanut butter sandwich for my lunch. My mom had to go to work early today."

Suddenly he sat upright and pointed. "See that mailbox, Mr. Harding? It's ours. Turn right, just after we pass it, on the dirt road. Our house is only a little ways in the woods there."

I did as I was told, driving along slowly and carefully on the narrow, rutted lane for perhaps a hundred yards before the beams of my headlights reflected off the front of a shabby wooden structure that looked like a storage area for wood or farm equipment. Many of the unpainted clapboards along the front of the shack were missing or cracked, and there was a large area, near one corner, where someone had nailed a large and unpainted square piece of plywood. A light shone from the uncurtained window to the left of the doorway, while more plywood was nailed across the window frame to the right. Off to the side, parked under several pine trees, was a rusting blue Renault sedan.

"That's my mom's car," Timothy explained. "She says it runs a lot better than it looks . . . and it does."

An uncovered, fly-specked light bulb shone above the front door, which opened slowly as a woman stepped out onto the landing, raising both her hands to cover her eyes. I immediately turned off my headlights. "That's my mom," Tim announced as we were both getting out of the car. I followed him to the steps, which were only cinder blocks piled loosely atop one another.

She was standing nervously and uncertainly just outside the door, grasping the doorknob with one hand and her apron with the other. "Good evening, Mrs. Noble. I'm Timothy's Little League manager, John Harding. Saw him walking home tonight, so I thought I'd give him a lift."

Her voice sounded both youthful and weary, which was probably a good description of her appearance as well. "That is so nice of you, Mr. Harding. Won't you please come in?"

I hesitated, feeling more than a little uncomfortable, but a glimpse of Timothy nodding hopefully up at me was not to be ignored. The door opened directly into the kitchen, and as soon as we were inside, Timothy's mother extended her right hand to me tentatively and said, "I'm Peggy Noble, sir, and I'm so glad for this opportunity to thank you in person for all that you have done for my son."

She wore little makeup, her blond hair needed brushing and combing and her face was slightly flushed. Two pans were on the stove emitting steam. Mrs. Noble was obviously preparing supper, but she said, "Please, Mr. Harding, have a seat," as she pulled a plastic-covered chair out from behind a small table that was already set for two. Beyond an old refrigerator, at the other side of the kitchen and close to the ceiling, I could see what looked like a piece of clothesline stretched across the room. Bedsheets hung from it as a sort of curtain, but they didn't quite conceal the two unmade beds, barely visible in the shadows beyond. Timothy and his mother, I immediately realized, were living in a one-room camp that probably, in bygone years, had been used only by hunters each fall.

"Have a seat, Mr. Harding," she repeated.

"No, thank you, Mrs. Noble. I've got to be going. Now, how about next week? Our first game is on Tuesday. Will Timothy have his bike back by then, or should I come by and pick him up?"

Her gray eyes filled with tears. "You are so kind, sir. So kind. No, they told me that I could pick up the bike this Saturday, so Timothy will be okay next week."

"Great! Then I'll be on my way. Didn't mean to disturb your supper, but it was still nice to meet you. This is a lucky boy to have you."

"I'm afraid I don't do so very much for him. It's hard, and I try because I love him so. But, Mr. Harding, most of all, he is lucky to have you in his life . . . at this time. So lucky. Thanks be to God you selected him."

She moved closer to me, stood on her toes and kissed my cheek.

I drove home very slowly.

X I

*L*ate Saturday afternoon, after stocking up on milk, bread, soda pop and frozen dinners at the local convenience store, I walked around the backyard that Bobby Compton and his crew had mowed and trimmed so neatly on Friday. Along both sides of the deck, pink Simplicity roses that Sally had planted so carefully, back in March when I thought it was still too early in the season, were now covered with blossoms. I snapped one off, inhaled its faint fragrance and pushed its thorny stem carefully into my shirt pocket. Then I strolled out into the meadow beyond our lawn to check on the wild-blueberry bushes. The clusters of berries were still pale green except for an occasional dab of pink. They were at least two or three weeks from picking, but even when ripe none of them would ever find their way into a Sally Harding pie or muffin or one of her giant blueberry turnovers that I remember holding in both hands, while still warm, before taking that first bite. Memories! Here I go again. All our lives, it seems, someone is trying to teach us how to remember better. There are even scores of memory courses and lectures on the subject, but I've never heard of a course on how to forget, and I'm certain that for some it would be a very popular seminar. Many of those who are so proud of their great ability to recall people and dates and events may well admit, someday, that their blessing has become a curse.

On Tuesday evening we gave Chuck Barrio the starting assignment against the Cubs, and the classy left-hander was almost perfect for four innings. We were leading 8 to 1 when the Cubs came to bat in the fifth inning and exploded for twelve runs. They scored seven runs off Chuck before I relieved him with Paul Taylor, since Todd was scheduled for the Thursday game against the Pirates. Paul didn't have it, either, walking the first three batters he faced before allowing two singles and a double. I blame myself for his poor performance, since I didn't insist that he warm up longer after we sent him to the mound, even though the umpire was willing. In any event, we let a game that was won get away from us. The final score was 15 to 9, Cubs. Ben Rogers, our silent man at shortstop, was our batting star with two doubles and a single, and Todd hit another home run. Since all the Angels were now well aware that Timothy was the only one on the team without a hit, they all agonized on every pitch when he went to bat in the fifth, but the little guy went down swinging, once again, to end the inning.

On Thursday, against Anthony Piso's Pirates, we had a field day. Todd pitched shutout ball, and we unloaded on four Pirate pitchers for fourteen runs, never scoring less than two in any inning. Although our guys made twenty hits, according to Bill West and his scorebook, they all seemed more concerned about Timothy getting his first one. All the time he was at the plate, in the fourth inning, our dugout sounded more like a huge concrete high-fidelity speaker blaring, "Never give up, never give up, Timothy, Timothy, never give up!" until the home-plate umpire finally called time, came over to our bench and asked the boys if they would all kindly lower their voices to no more than a loud roar so that his calls could be heard. Our Angels stood and applauded as he walked back to the plate before renewing their cheers for Timothy. He did get his bat on one pitch and hit a fairly hard line drive down the right-field line that was foul, but then he missed the next two pitches. When he tossed his bat toward our dugout and ran out to his position in right, Bill beckoned to me to sit next to him.

"What's up?" I asked.

"Timothy. Does he seem okay to you?"

"Yeah, why?"

"I don't know. He looks even more pale than usual, and when he ran in from the outfield, after the last inning, he acted as if he was having a tough time just keeping his balance. I asked him if he felt okay, and he just nodded his head."

When the game ended, after we had exchanged congratulations with the Pirates at home plate, I made it a point to talk with him. "Timothy, how's the new bike chain?"

He nodded vigorously. "Great. It's like I have new wheels."

The words were spoken as individual utterances, with long pauses between each, not as a single, total sentence. Strange.

"Are you feeling okay?"

He nodded again. "I'm a little tired. My mom had to go to work early today and I heard her making breakfast, so I woke up."

I patted him softly on the head. "Get a good night's sleep tonight, you hear?"

He nodded and forced a half smile. "Good night, Mr. Harding."

Bill's car was parked next to mine in the parking lot. He was leaning against his vehicle, waiting for me, a concerned look on his face. "What did you find out, John . . . about Timothy?"

I shrugged my shoulders. "He said he was tired because he was accidentally awakened early by his mother, but, I don't know, his voice pattern sounds a little weird, like someone speaking while they are under hypnosis."

Bill sighed. "The most amazing thing to me, John, is that the kid is still playing at all. I've coached a lot of Little League kids through the years, and when they keep striking out and do little or nothing very good in the field, they will usually quit, after a few games, rather than continue to be embarrassed by their lack of ability or coordination. Not this boy! He comes to play every day, hustles all the time, tries his very best, asks for no sympathy and instead of moping at his own failures he cheers loudest of all for every one of his teammates. That is one brave little Angel. We can all learn a hell of a lot from him."

We can all learn a hell of a lot from him. I kept hearing Bill's words, over and over, long after I had put out the light and crawled into bed.

The mid-July afternoon was hot and muggy, and huge waves of cumulus clouds were gathering overhead when I pulled into the Little League parking lot for our important Monday game against Sid Marx and his Yankees. After having completed half of our twelve-game schedule, we now shared the league lead with the Yankees, having both won four and lost two, while the Pirates and Cubs had each won two and lost four.

In the lot, parked next to Bill's car was a white panel truck with red lettering on both sides and the rear doors: NEW HAMPSHIRE'S LEADING TELEVISION STATION—CHANNEL 9—WMUR-TV—MANCHESTER, N.H. I didn't give it another thought until I stepped through the opening in the fence and onto the grass and saw two young men in blue jeans and T-shirts fussing over a tripod and television camera that was facing toward the first-base dugout, our dugout for the game, as we were the designated visiting team. Another young man, in a dark business suit, who had been standing behind the camera, looked up as I approached and said, "Here he is now, guys. Perfect timing."

"Mr. Harding," he said as he extended his hand and smiled, "I'm Tom Land, one of the sportscasters at Channel Nine in Manchester. We'd like to interview you for our *Eleven O'Clock News* this evening, if you don't mind. Our station has already cleared it with your league president, Mr. Rand."

"Why in the world would you want to interview me? There are hundreds of Little League managers in New Hampshire, and if you want to talk with a real good one, he's probably already in that other dugout. His name is Sid Marx. Great coach, and the kids love him."

"Well, sir," he said, nodding his head, "there may be hundreds of other Little League managers and coaches in this state, but I promise you that none is as well known in New Hampshire, and the nation, as John Harding. I doubt there are many of our viewers who are not familiar with how you rose to become president and chief executive officer of Millennium Unlimited at such an early age before . . . before . . ."

He stared at the ground, finally forced a smile and said, "And now, to see such a celebrated American example of success coaching a small-town Little League team instead of running that Fortune 500 corporation, gosh it's an unbelievable story. I'm glad we found you before the networks!"

"Well, now, whom do you want to interview, John

Harding, manager of the Angels or . . . or John Harding, former and very brief chief executive officer of mighty Millennium?"

Deep furrows suddenly appeared in his wide forehead. "Why . . . why . . . both!" he stammered.

"I'm sorry, but I'm going to pass."

He acted as if he hadn't heard me. "Mr. Harding, it won't take us very long. Perhaps ten minutes. I have just a few questions I want to ask you, questions that I'm certain our audience would like to hear you answer, such as how you have handled the past few months, since the terrible tragedy, and then perhaps some questions comparing the old days of Little League when you were an all-star right here, on this very field, with the conditions and players of today."

"Mr. Land, we're trying to get ourselves ready to play a ball game. I thank you and your fine television station for this honor, but my answer is no, and I'm afraid you and your people will have to move that camera and pretty damn quickly. As you can see, my kids are starting to arrive, and that thing is exactly the kind of distraction they don't need. Now, if you care to shoot some of the game, be my guest. Back there, behind the home-plate wire backstop, you will find a handsome old boy named George McCord. He's our public-address announcer, and I'm sure he'll be glad to show you where you can best set up your camera." I extended my hand. "Nice to meet you, Mr. Land."

He stared at me in disbelief, his mouth partially open. "You mean you won't do the interview?"

I patted his shoulder. "Correct! Now, kindly move your camera so that these kids can get themselves ready to play ball."

It was a tough game. With Channel 9's camera stationed in the stands behind third base, the Angels and Yankees both played as if their very lives hung in the balance. Our guys took an early 2-to-0 lead in the second inning when Bob Murphy tripled to deep center, scoring Zullo and Nurnberg, but the Yankees came back in the fourth with four straight hits after Paul Taylor had some control trouble, and we were down 4 to 2. We managed to score one more in the sixth, but the losing final score was a bitter pill to swallow, 4 to 3. Tank Kimball finally found his batting eye, collecting two singles and a double, and Timothy came to bat with two men on in the fifth and a chance to be a hero. I found myself saying silent prayers, asking God to please let him get a hit, just a single, as if God had nothing more to worry about than a small-town Little League game. Later in the evening, recalling that moment, I would realize that it was the first prayer of any kind I had said since the funeral.

After swinging wildly at the first two pitches, Tim refused to bite at the next two, which were both over his head, before he dug in with both feet, swung and connected. It was only an infield pop fly to the third-baseman, but he had finally hit a ball in fair territory during a game, and our entire team leaped to their feet, applauding and shouting as Timothy stepped on first base before he turned to jog back to the dugout. He paused, halfway back, doffed his cap and waved it toward the television camera behind third base before taking his seat on the bench. I was watching him carefully. When he came down the dugout steps, he seemed to be swaying from side to side and he was breathing hard. Then, when he went to sit, he first reached toward the bench with both hands before he lowered himself onto the wood.

We bounced back on Wednesday evening against the lowly Cubs. Everyone in our lineup—that is, everyone except Timothy—managed to get at least one hit, and three of our guys had perfect nights, three for three! Final score was 13 to 4. Todd experimented with a few new pitches, including a knuckleball his older brother was using successfully in high school, or I'm certain he would have had another shutout. Timothy took some good cuts, but went down swinging on four pitches. He did, however, finally catch his first fly ball of the year, a fairly well hit ball that went right at him. He just held up his new glove and caught it as any major-leaguer would. Of course that produced another chorus of cheers from all the Angels, whether they were in the field or on the bench, and gave him another chance to doff his cap. What a little ham! And when he arrived in the dugout, he shouted, "Day by day, in every way, I'm really and truly getting better and better!"

Now, with only four games remaining, the Yankees had a record of six wins and two losses, and we were second with five wins and three losses. Since the top two teams would play a single game at the conclusion of the season, for the league championship, I would have been satisfied if the regular season had ended right then. But we still had four more to play, and both the Pirates, with three wins and five losses, and even the Cubs, with two wins and six losses, could possibly catch us. We couldn't relax yet.

. . . And Timothy Noble, still without a base hit, was running out of games.

XII

Most New England towns fire off as large a display of fireworks as they can afford, usually on their most spacious athletic field, in celebration of Independence Day. Not the township of Boland. Of course most of its citizens drive to nearby Concord to enjoy fireworks displays on July Fourth, but then they have their own special celebration. Since town hall records show that Boland's first settler, Isaac Thomas Boland, arrived among unfriendly animals and natives on July 17, 1735, that was the day when most of the townspeople always gathered in the grandstand and parking lot of Boland Little League Park. When darkness fell, rockets, Roman candles and a varied assortment of aerial bombshells were launched from the outfield area, exploding high above in a noisy and brilliant spectrum of blazing colors while the crowd "oohed" and screamed and applauded.

Since July 17th fell on a Monday, our scheduled
games, normally played Monday through Thursday each
week, were all moved ahead a day, and our game against
the Pirates was listed for Tuesday evening. Bill had
phoned, sometime in mid-afternoon on Monday, asking
if I wanted to go to the fireworks with him and Edy. I
thanked him but declined. After some pastrami on rye
with a glass of skim milk for supper, I went out on the
deck, settled into my favorite chaise lounge and had almost dozed off when the first aerial bombshell exploded, almost directly over the house. Startled, I
looked up just in time to see scores of flaming stars of
all colors falling lazily out of a swirling pillar of white
smoke. I sat up and watched as glowing rockets and
bright balls of light climbed, one after the other, high
into the heavens, arching up from the playing field a
half mile or so away, which was hidden from view by
tall pines and oaks.

After several minutes it became very difficult for me
to watch. Almost from Rick's infancy, fireworks had fas-
cinated him. From the time he was only three, back in
Santa Clara, and then for the two years in Denver, Sally
and I had always taken him to see "the works!" on each
Fourth of July. I remember holding him on my knees for
the first couple of years. He would bounce up and down
constantly while the rockets soared higher and higher,
his big blue eyes opened so wide that there were deep
furrows in his forehead as he pointed upward with the
forefingers of both hands and shrieked his appreciation
of each swishing rocket when it exploded to discharge

multicolored stars and glowing balls of magnesium while the odor of burning sulphur and charcoal filled the summer air.

I watched the Boland township's celebration of lights in the sky for perhaps twenty minutes. It was probably the loneliest twenty minutes of my life. Then I went into the house and climbed into bed, hoping that I would never awake.

Our kids were obviously getting a little cockier with each game and there was already talk of the big championship game against the Yankees, even though Bill and I kept reminding them that they hadn't clinched anything yet. On Tuesday evening the whole team seemed higher than a kite at batting practice, and they were teasing Timothy because he had arrived wearing a brand-new pair of white Nike baseball shoes with molded cleats of black and red. When he saw me, he came running over and said, "See my new shoes, Mr. Harding."

"They look great! How do you like them?"

He nodded eagerly. "They're nice. Doc Messenger took me to Concord this morning and bought them for me. He said my old sneakers were no good to play ball in!"

With that he turned and ran to the outfield, arms pumping furiously, straining to land on his toes with each step like the most graceful of runners.

Our game against the Pirates began as a real pitchers' duel. For the first two innings neither team was able to get the ball out of the infield, and Paul Taylor was throwing harder than I had ever seen him throw. Then, as swiftly as the wind can change directions here in New England, the game turned into a wild slugfest after both Todd and Tank hit home runs, back to back, in the third inning and our guys followed by scoring seven more. Tony Piso and his boys came right back with six of their own when Paul lost his control in the fourth inning, although I did let him stay in the game and he finally got the side out.

In the fifth inning, as Timothy was walking to the plate, his teammates commenced their chanting, "Timothy, Timothy, never give up, never give up!" Then they began clapping their hands in rhythm, and soon the crowd directly behind our dugout started to clap until the entire grandstand had joined in. Everyone was rooting for the little guy to get his first hit. He tried. Oh, how he tried! Looked good at the plate, took smooth cuts at the ball, but . . . he struck out on three pitches as the crowd groaned their disappointment.

We did finally win the game, sloppy as it was, 14 to 9.

He was leaning against the trunk of an old Jaguar sedan, parked next to my car in the parking lot, and although he didn't need to introduce himself because I recognized him, he did anyway.

"Mr. Harding," he said, smiling and extending a large hand, "I'm Doc Messenger. When someone told me that I was parked next to your buggy, I couldn't pass up the opportunity to hang around long enough to tell you how much I admire you, your courage and the great way you handle your team. Kids always see right through phony adults, and it's obvious that the Angels respect you and enjoy playing for you."

"Thank you, sir. Much appreciated. I'm so glad to finally meet the legendary Doc Messenger after all I've heard about you. Timothy Noble talks about you often. He's a lucky kid to have you keeping an eye on him."

The old man folded his arms, smiled, and replied in a deep baritone voice, "Well, I don't know about that. What I do know, for sure, is how fortunate he is to be playing for a man like you."

"Doc, is Timothy okay? Sometimes he seems to lose his balance, and other times he looks as if he's in pain when he runs, but he says he isn't."

He stroked his long white beard several times before replying, "He's okay. Just a few childhood problems, but I'm keeping an eye on him. I've even come to all your games."

"Day by day, in every way . . ."

He smiled. "The little fellow has really taken to those old self-motivators, hasn't he? I only taught him two, but they seem to keep him positive and with a good outlook on life, even if they haven't produced a hit as yet. Amazing and powerful tools, self-motivators. They could be a miracle treatment for so many if only we could get more people to believe in that mysterious power contained in simple words. All we have to do is program our subconscious mind with positive thoughts and words, and when we do, we can work wonders in our lives. So many of us, perhaps all of us, talk to ourselves throughout the day anyway, so why not feed ourselves positive words and ideas that are beneficial. 'I can win, I can get the job done, I can make the sale' are just as easy to say as 'I can't win, I can't complete the job, I'll never make the sale.' Norman Vincent Peale, W. Clement Stone, Napoleon Hill, Maxwell Maltz and so many other great minds have tried to teach us this simple technique to change our lives for the better. Self-affirmations, employed by man or woman to improve production, behavior and even thinking have been used successfully for thousands of years. Did you know that Epictetus, the old Roman philosopher, even offered us special words to help us deal with the terrible loss of a loved one? He said, 'Never say about anything, I have lost it, but only I have given it back. Is your child dead? He has been given back. Is your wife dead? She has been returned.' " He leaned over and patted my shoulder. "Keep up the good work, Mr. Harding. I'm so glad we had this chat." Then he turned and unlocked the door of his car, and I turned toward mine, unable to say anything.

Thursday's game against Sid Marx and his Yankees turned out to be another nail biter, with Todd Stevenson pitching against their best, Glenn Gerston. No one reached third base, on either side, until Justin Nurnberg cracked a double between left and center field that rolled all the way to the fence, and then he advanced on

Paul Taylor's infield grounder to second. However, we couldn't bring our man home, so we had a scoreless tie on our hands as we began the fourth inning with the top of the Yankee batting order coming to the plate. Todd struck out the first two, but then he walked the next, and Sid's cleanup batter followed with a line drive down the left-field line that kept rising and rising until it disappeared over the fence, and we were suddenly trailing by two. The next batter, after fouling several pitches, hit a high fly to right field, and Bill West, sitting next to me, buried his head in his hands and groaned until the crowd roared and nearly everyone rose to their feet as Timothy, after making a fine two-handed catch as I had taught him, came jogging into the bench while the crowd applauded. Then he glanced over toward me and shouted, "Nothing to it!"

At the plate things were not so productive for Timothy. After fouling off several pitches, he finally went down swinging. Actually none of our bats were very potent against Gerston, and we suffered our third defeat against only one victory for the year against the Yankees.

On the following Monday, with Chuck Barrio on the mound for us, we handled the Cubs easily, 17 to 5, and that win clinched second place in the league, which meant that a week from Saturday we would tangle once more with the Yankees, this time for the league championship. Ben Rogers and Bob Murphy both had three hits, and Tank poked another home run in our lopsided victory. I let Andros, Lang and Noble play the entire final four innings, and Timothy got to bat twice since all our guys were really pounding the ball. He struck out both times, but both times he came back to the bench with head still held high. What a special kid!

While our team was running out onto the field for the sixth inning, Bill West came over to where I was standing and asked softly, "Have you heard about Timothy?"

"No. What's wrong?"

"Well, the kids were telling me that his bike is out of commission again. Apparently the new chain his mother bought snapped on the way here today, so I guess he just left the old thing by the side of the road and ran the last couple of miles to be here on time. How's that for desire?"

After the game, as we were loading the equipment into the trunk of Bill's car, I called to Timothy as he trotted by.

"Yes, sir?"

"How about a ride home?"

He sighed, and dragged his new shoes in the sand. "Someone told you about my stupid bike?"

"Yup."

We had been riding for perhaps ten minutes before the little guy exclaimed, "This isn't the way home."

"It is for me."

"We're going to your house? Why?"

"Wait and see. We'll be there in a couple of minutes."

I finally turned into my driveway, drove up the grade, pushed the button on my garage-door opener and waited until the door was all the way up and the lights had turned on.

"Timothy, jump out for a minute. There's something I want to show you."

He followed me uncertainly into the garage. I walked over to where Rick's new red Huffy "Street Rocker" bicycle was hanging on one of the walls, suspended by two large metal brackets. Holding my breath, I reached up to feel both tires and was relieved when they felt hard. Then I grasped the frame in both hands and lifted Rick's last birthday present from its place on the wall. I lowered it to the concrete floor, in front of Timothy, and said, "This is yours. It's not giving enjoyment to anyone, just hanging there, and I'm sure Rick would want you to have it if he knew you."

Timothy's two tiny hands moved slowly across the chrome handle bars and down the dusty but bright frame. "It's brand-new, Mr. Harding!"

"Yes, just about."

"Is it really mine, forever, or just until baseball is over?"

"It's yours forever and ever."

"Wow!" he exclaimed, "I'll take good care of it, honest I will."

"I know you will. Now it's almost dark, so let's put the bike in my trunk and I'll drive you home. Then tomorrow you can start riding it, okay?"

He nodded eagerly. "It's the first new bike I've ever owned, Mr. Harding!"

When we pulled up close to Timothy's home, the outside light did not go on.

"I don't think my mom is home from work yet. Her car isn't here."

I removed the bike from the trunk and leaned it against the side of the house where clapboards were missing.

"Will you be okay?" I asked.

"Oh, yes, my mom will be home soon. Do you know what she promised, Mr. Harding?"

"No, what?"

"She said that if we got to play in the championship game next Saturday, she would take the day off, even if her boss got mad at her, and come to see me play. Won't that be neat?"

"It certainly will be."

"She's never seen me play. Did you know that? Maybe I'll get a hit in that game, while she's watching."

"I sure do hope so, Timothy. Now, don't forget Wednesday night's game, the last one before the big one. We're playing the Pirates, and we can all start getting ourselves ready, in that game, for the championship tussle. Okay? See you Wednesday."

"Yes, sir. Thank you, Mr. Harding. Thank you."

I guess our kids were already looking ahead to the championship game against the Yankees, a week from Saturday, because they were terrible in their final game against the Pirates. I pitched Todd for three innings and

Paul Taylor for three so that my two aces would have some work in preparation for the big one, but the team as a whole played a sloppy game, and I think we managed to squeak out an 11-to-10 victory because the Pirates, certain to finish third in the league standings no matter what the outcome of our game, played as if they didn't care.

Since we had clinched our spot in the championship game, I let Timothy play the entire six innings, hoping he would get that base hit he wanted so badly. He did hit a hard grounder to the pitcher in the second inning, but then he went down swinging the other two times he batted.

The ballpark and parking lot were nearly empty by the time Bill and I had gathered all the baseball gear and piled it into the trunk of his car. In the twilight I moved close to my old friend, extended my hand and said softly, "I'll never be able to repay you for what you have done for me."

Bill cocked his head and frowned. "What are you saying, John?"

"You came back into my life at just the right time. You gave me something to worry about, to think about, to live for—the Angels. You and those great kids actually returned my life to me when I didn't want one anymore. God bless you."

We embraced and said good night. However, when I was perhaps twenty feet away, walking toward my car, Bill called after me. I turned.

"Maybe we all contributed a little bit, John," he called

out, "but you had better not forget to thank our smallest Angel. He's taught all of us how to deal with life, day by day."

I don't remember how long I sat in my car before I turned the key in the ignition.

XIII

$\mathcal{D}$uring what seemed like an agonizingly long week leading up to the championship game on Saturday afternoon, we held two practice sessions for our Angels on Monday and Wednesday afternoons, while Sid Marx put his Yankees through their paces on Tuesday and Thursday. We concentrated on basics, especially batting, and although the kids were in great spirits, I couldn't say the same for Bill and myself. Following the final game of the regular season we had learned from Paul Taylor's mother that he would not be available for the championship game. Plans had been made and hotel rooms reserved by the Taylors almost a year ago to take Paul to Bermuda for two weeks of golf and scuba diving, and unfortunately their scheduled departure was just a day before the big game. As Paul's mother said, "Who knew, ten months ago, that our son would be needed to help win a ball game—the championship game?" However, before Monday's practice, Paul's smiling dad came over to Bill and me with the joyful news that he had managed to postpone his vacation for a week as well as change the family's reservation dates at the exclusive Sonesta Beach Hotel. A miracle! Neither Bill nor I could believe our good luck.

The big game was scheduled to begin at two P.M. on Saturday, but when I arrived, slightly before one P.M., the stands were almost filled to capacity and people had already started to open their folding chairs in both the left- and right-field foul territory, a custom that had apparently been initiated many years ago for the annual championship tussle. In the grandstands, to add to the special flavor and ambience of baseball on a warm summer afternoon, two vendors dressed in white were already busy selling ice-cream bars and boxes of popcorn. Behind home plate George McCord was doing his best to get the crowd into the spirit of the day by playing college marching songs over the loudspeakers, with the volume turned up a little bit louder than usual.

Bill saw me as soon as I came through the fence opening onto the field, and he immediately came jogging over. "Couple of things, John," he said as he wiped the perspiration from his forehead. "Over there, behind home plate," he said without looking in that direction, "are some reporters—from the *Concord Monitor* and the *Manchester Union Leader.*"

"For a Little League game? This isn't for the state championship, for God's sake!"

"No. They said they were here to observe how a billion-dollar executive manages a bunch of kids under thirteen."

"Great! Just what I need."

"They're nice guys. Not to worry."

I glanced around the playing field. Four Angels had already arrived. Tony Zullo was playing catch with Timothy, and Paul Taylor was fielding grounders that Justin was rolling to him from his first-base position. "Bill, what else did you want to tell me?

"Well, I thought you'd like to know that Timothy's mother did come. She's sitting in the first row of seats behind the third-base dugout, with Doc Messenger. Wearing a white T-shirt and a pink hat."

"I see her. Thanks, Bill."

I walked over to the stands, removed my Angel baseball cap and extended my right hand. "Mrs. Noble . . . Doc . . . I'm glad you are both here. I know this means a lot to Timothy."

Mrs. Noble smiled and nodded. "Nothing could have kept me away today, Mr. Harding. Nothing. I hope you win."

"Thank you. Doc, it's good to see you again."

The old man nodded as he shook my hand. "It's mutual, sir. Mr. Harding, if you would, please refresh my fading memory for me. Am I correct that Timothy has yet to achieve his first hit of the season?"

"Yes, I'm sorry to say it's true."

The old man removed his battered cowboy hat

and stared at it. "This game, then, is his last opportunity."

"Yes, I'm afraid so, for this year anyway, and it won't be easy. The Yankees are throwing their ace pitcher at us, and he's very tough for anyone to hit."

"Well," he said softly, "I wish you the very best for your team, and I guess we'll just have to pray extra hard when our young man comes to the plate."

"Thank you," I said, turning back toward the field as the familiar strains of the "Notre Dame Marching Song" echoed through the ballpark.

On a folding bridge table, behind home plate's heavy wire backstop, Stewart Rand and Nancy McLaren had placed twenty-four trophies that sparkled in the bright sun, each a golden life-size baseball mounted on a square wooden base that held a small metal plaque already engraved with each player's name, team, and the words BOLAND LITTLE LEAGUE CHAMPIONSHIP GAME. There were no losers in our league.

Finally two umpires approached home plate and beckoned to Sid and me. The tall one, Jake Laughlin, would be umpiring at home, and the other blue shirt, on the bases, was Tim Spelling.

"Gentlemen," Laughlin said hoarsely, "this is the only Little League game played here, all season, where the home team is not designated by the league schedule. Mr. Marx, I'm going to flip this quarter. While it's in the air, will you kindly call heads or tails? In this toss there are no options. The winner of the toss will be considered the home team, bat last, and have the third-base dugout, understood?"

We both nodded, and while the coin was still above our heads, Sid yelled, "Tails!"

Another stroke of good luck. The familiar profile of George Washington stared up at us. My Angels would bat last. Fortunately our guys had already dropped most of their equipment and gloves in the third-base dugout as if they were unafraid to tempt fate, so they all cheered lustily when I told them they could stay and that we had last "ups" at bat. After they were all seated, except Todd, who was warming up behind our dugout, I walked slowly from one end of our bench to the other, my hands in my back pockets, leaning slightly so that I could look into the eyes of each boy. Finally I said, "Well, you made it to the big game, and each of you should be proud of the important part you played in the success of the Angels. Now, I have just one thing to say to all of you. Yes, this is the big one, but I want everyone to have fun today. That's what this is all about. Being here today is your reward for your efforts all season, but rewards aren't much good if you can't laugh and smile and enjoy them. Remember, the sun will still rise tomorrow, whether you win or lose, and your best years are still ahead of you. Sure, it would be nice to win, but this is not life or death. It's just a ball game, so stay loose, enjoy the day and remember what Timothy Noble has been telling us all season." I pointed toward the little guy. "Remind them once more, Tim."

He stood, raised his small arms above his head,

clenched those tiny fists and yelled, "Never give up, never give up, never give up!" Immediately the entire team joined in, "Never give up, never give up, never give up!"

The tall ump was waving at both dugouts and pointing toward the foul lines running from home plate. The Angels raced out onto the field and took their single-file positions down the third-base foul line, while the Yankees did the same down the first-base line, both teams close to home plate. Following an upbeat rendition of the national anthem that George McCord played over the loudspeakers, Todd walked out to the pitching mound, but this time, as previously arranged, he was joined by Yankee ace, Glenn Gerston, and together the two of them led the others in reciting the Little League Pledge. Then the home-plate umpire raised his mask high above his head, and our Angels leaped from the dugout shouting, "Never give up, never, never, never!" as they ran to their positions on the field.

The forty-fourth annual Boland Little League Championship game was about to begin.

Following Bill West's suggestion, I had asked Todd Stevenson to warm up for at least ten minutes more than he usually did to prepare for a game, and the tall blond was faster than I had ever seen him. He opened the game by striking out the first two Yankees to face him. Then he walked the third batter before the Yankees cleanup slugger smashed a double to deep left-center and the Yankees suddenly had runners on second and third, bringing up their pitcher, Gerston. Todd worked very carefully on his opposite number until the count was three balls and two strikes before Gerston swung at a fast inside pitch and cracked a hard shot between first and second and we were suddenly behind by two runs before we nailed down the final out of the inning.

In our half of the first, although Tony Zullo walked to lead things off, Justin and Paul hit easy grounders to the infield and Todd went down swinging after hitting two balls over the left-field fence—both foul.

We managed to retire the Yankees in order in the second inning but they did the same to us after both Tank and Charles Barrio walked. Opportunity wasted. Then, as Bill and I had planned, we inserted our other three Angels into the lineup at the top of the third inning. Chris Lang went in for Tony Zullo at second, Dick Andros went to left, replacing Bob Murphy, and Timothy Noble jogged out to right, replacing Jeff Gaston.

Sid Marx also made several changes. His scorekeeper and Bill exchanged the names of each team's substitute, near home plate, after they had both notified the game's official scorekeeper, who was seated at another folding table next to Nancy and the trophies, behind the wire backstop.

The first Yankee batter in the third inning smashed one of Todd's fastballs down the third-base line, just inside the bag. I still don't know how our Paul Taylor managed to get to the ball, but he did, making a sensational diving backhand catch before falling to the ground. The crowd leaped to its feet, applauding and cheering for at least five minutes before both umpires went to the pitching mound and raised their arms, until the appreciative fans reluctantly settled back in their seats. It had been one of the finest baseball plays I had ever seen. Todd then struck out the next batter, and the side was retired when their lanky catcher hit a towering fly to center field, which Charles Barrio handled easily. Both teams, so far, had played errorless ball despite the pressure of the championship, but the Yankees had a two-run lead as we came to bat in the bottom of the third inning.

Standing behind third, in the coach's box, I was beginning to feel a little desperate. Gerston was pitching a great game, and he showed no sign of weakening. We needed to force a break of some kind. As our lead-off batter, Chris Lang, walked toward the plate, I flashed him the bunt sign when he looked my way. He let the first pitch go, for a called strike, then dropped a near-perfect bunt down the third-base line, but it wasn't good enough. He was out—by just a half step. Justin Nurnberg was our next batter. I was tempted to flash another bunt sign but didn't. He hit a slow dribbler to the pitcher's right which Gerston fielded smoothly in time to catch Justin, again by no more than a half step. Paul Taylor glanced in my direction anxiously as he stepped into the batter's box. I flashed him no signs. Good thing. He caught Gerston's second pitch, an inside fastball, and drilled it high over the left-field fence for a home run! Now we were only down by one run. Todd was the next batter, and he hit a drive to center, but it wasn't long enough, and the inning was over with the Yankees still leading us, two to one.

In the fourth inning Todd seemed to be throwing even harder than in the early innings. No Yankee hitter got the ball out of the infield. Three up, three down.

"Kimball, Barrio and Andros," Bill said loudly, announcing our first three scheduled batters as the Angels came into the dugout. "Let's get 'em guys! Now! Big inning!" he shouted as he walked up and down the dugout floor, tapping each Angel lightly on top of his cap.

"Never give up!" shouted Timothy, and the others immediately joined in. "Never give up, never give up!"

Tank led off by drawing a walk. If it had been anyone but Tank, I would have tried to move him along with a sacrifice bunt, but the big guy was just too slow, so I had Charles Barrio hit away. He hit a hard grounder to the shortstop, who fielded it cleanly, flipped the ball to the second-baseman, who then turned and threw to first. Double play! Dick Andros followed with a swinging strikeout, and we were still trailing by a single run going into the fifth inning.

As the first Yankee scheduled to bat, in the fifth, was selecting his bat from the rack, Sid jogged by, close to our dugout, on his way to the third-base coaching box.

"Hey, John!" he yelled.

"Yes, Sid?"

"It doesn't get much better than this, does it? Great kids! Both teams!"

I smiled and nodded.

The first Yankee batter attempted a bunt, but he popped the ball into the air, and Todd caught it easily. The next batter, a short and very muscular left-hander who played first base for Sid's team, took two called strikes before he swung at an inside pitch and smashed a hard line drive to right field, directly at Timothy.

"Oh, no!" I heard Bill cry, but Timothy raised his glove above his head, turned his feet slightly so that his right foot was a brace for his small frame, and the sound of the ball popping into his new glove could be heard throughout the entire park, which had momentarily grown very quiet. When the crowd realized that Timothy had caught the ball, they rose to their feet, cheering. Timothy just smiled and nodded as he flipped the ball back in to Justin at first base. The next Yankee struck out, and now the Angels were coming to bat. The first three batters, according to Bill's announcement, would be Rogers, Noble and Lang.

Glenn Gerston showed no signs of tiring, and he was still throwing strikes for the Yankees. But our Ben Rogers surprised us. He managed to work the count to two balls and two strikes before he caught a waist-high fastball and hit a smash into left-center between outfielders. Although I knew the play would be close, since the centerfielder had already retrieved the ball, I waved Ben toward me as he raced around second, and held my breath as both runner and ball converged at third base. Ben made a perfect hook slide, and the sweep of the third-baseman's glove, holding the ball, just missed his right foot. "Safe!" yelled the umpire, and the stands erupted in a crescendo of noise and whistles as Timothy Noble walked slowly to the plate with the tying run only sixty feet away!

The little guy paused, perhaps ten feet from the batter's box, scooped up a handful of dirt and rubbed his hands in it. He turned and looked toward me. I flashed the "hit away" sign. He nodded. Then he stepped into the box very slowly, pulled up his pants, tugged on the visor of his cap and assumed his batting stance. It was then that both Bill West and I witnessed something we had never seen before, even back in our own playing days. All the Angels were now standing and leaning forward, their elbows on top of the dugout wall, staring intently out at Timothy. In silence! In complete silence, almost as if they were all praying! Suddenly the entire grandstand also grew very still, so still that one could even hear a train whistle in distant Concord.

Timothy cocked his bat several times, waiting. Gerston glanced over at Ben, standing on third base, before he went into an elaborate windup and tossed a slow ball to Timothy that almost floated on its way to the catcher. Timothy grinned and stepped out of the batter's box. Ball one!

Back in the box Timothy cocked his bat, crouched and waited. Gerston's next pitch was a fastball, right down the middle. Timothy let it go. Strike one! The next pitch was another fastball. Strike two! I turned and stole a glance at Mrs. Noble and Doc. Both were staring down at their hands as if they were unable to bring themselves to watch the action at home plate. The next pitch was another slow ball that Timothy ignored. He stepped out of the batter's box. Ball two. Now the count was two and two! Timothy moved slowly back into the box, tapped his bat on the plate, cocked it behind his shoulder and waited. Gerston's pitch, after another long windup, was belt-high and across the center of the plate. Timothy swung. His bat made solid contact! The ball bounced on the grass once, to Gerston's left, then it dribbled across the unseeded surface between first and second, barely eluding the first-baseman's sweeping glove as it rolled slower and slower toward the right-fielder, who was racing in to field the ball. Ben Rogers scored the tying run easily, from third, and Timothy was standing proudly with both his feet on first base! There was a look on his face that I shall never forget as he flashed a wide smile and raised his cap triumphantly above his head. He looked over at me and waved, then he turned and waved toward his mother and Doc, who were both standing and applauding along with everyone else in the park.

Now the top of our batting order was coming up, the score was tied and there were no outs! Sid Marx called time and walked slowly out to the pitcher's mound to talk with Glenn and his infield. While waiting, I walked back to our dugout from my coaching spot at third. Our next batter, Chris Lang, was waiting to move into the batter's box, but he ran back to join Nurnberg, Taylor and Stevenson as they gathered around me.

"Guys," I said, "I think this is it. Swing those bats nice and loose, just as you've been doing all year, and something tells me you'll win yourself a championship. Then you can have the rest of the summer off, okay? No lawn mowing. No weeding the family garden. No chores. How's that?"

They all grinned and nodded as the tall home-plate umpire exclaimed, "Let's play ball, gentlemen, what do you say?"

Sid patted his pitcher on the shoulder and jogged back to the dugout.

Chris Lang took his place in the batter's box as the umpire pulled on his face mask and yelled, "Play ball!"

Lang swung at the first pitch, hitting a high fly ball to left field that was caught on the run. One out. Timothy Noble, our go-ahead run, was still standing on first base.

Justin Nurnberg appeared overeager. He swung at the first two pitches even though they were well below his knees, but the third pitch was up around his chin, and he punched it into right field for a single, advancing Timothy to second base. The next batter, Paul Taylor, worked the count to a full three balls and two strikes before hitting a hard grounder to second base, but the only play was to first, so Timothy advanced to third, and Justin slid into second, bringing Todd Stevenson to the plate with two out.

Todd took hard rips at the first two pitches and missed both. Then he stepped out of the batter's box, inhaled deeply several times, stepped back in and stroked Gerston's next pitch over second base for a single, scoring Timothy with the go-ahead run and advanc-

ing Justin to third. Unfortunately Tank flied out to right
to end the fifth inning, but now we were ahead for the
first time, we were just three outs away from winning
the league championship, and Timothy Noble had
driven in the tying run plus scored the go-ahead run!

As our team took the field, I accompanied Todd out
to the pitcher's mound. "How's the arm, big guy?" I
asked, trying not to sound concerned.

He nodded, and wiped the perspiration from his
brow. "It's okay. Okay."

I rubbed his right shoulder gently. "Does it have three
more outs in there?"

He nodded again, unsmiling. "It's okay. Honest."

The first Yankee batter worked the count to three and
two before hitting a high fly ball to left field. One out!
Todd then walked the following batter on four pitches.
The next went down swinging. We needed only one
more out—but the top of the Yankee lineup was coming
up. Their leadoff man stroked four line-drive foul balls
down the left-field line before finally working Todd for
a base on balls. Now the Yankees had the tying run on
second and the winning run on first!

Bill West, sitting at my right, said quietly, "Boss, I
think you ought to go out there and have a little chat
with our man, right now."

I jumped to my feet, called "time" and walked slowly
out to the mound. Todd, with his back to the plate, was
staring down at the ground, pounding his glove inces-
santly against his right thigh.

"How are you feeling, buddy?" I asked.

"Fine. Fine."

"A little weary, maybe?"

"Nope. I'm okay. Honest."

"This guy coming up is pretty good with the stick. Can you get him?"

He just nodded. I patted him on the shoulder and jogged back to the dugout.

Todd stepped to the rubber, turned, took a fleeting look at the runner on second and quickly threw a belt-high fastball across the center of the plate.

"Strike one!"

Tank plucked the ball from his catcher's mitt, waved it above his head and tossed it back to Todd. With no windup, Todd immediately planted his left foot and fired the second pitch to a very surprised batter and catcher.

"Strike two!"

Bill turned to me, smiling. "See what Todd is doing, John? He's afraid you might take him out of the game, so he's working as fast as he can to get the Yankees out before you can get your duff off this bench and replace him."

Tank, now also sensing what his battery mate was up to, this time settled down into his catching position before flipping the ball back to Todd. Again Todd quickly reared back, with no windup, and fired his fastball across the heart of the plate.

"Strike three!"

We win!

Whistling and screaming, our kids dashed for the

pitcher's mound, where Todd was raised on small shoulders and proudly paraded around the bases as the Angels chanted, "We never gave up, we never gave up!" The entire crowd was now on its feet and applauding. Then, as the team approached third base, another figure was suddenly lifted on high to join Todd—Timothy! With both fists clenched, he pumped his small arms up and down while his teammates raised his small body as high as they could.

When the Angels finally arrived at home plate, they returned their two game heroes to earth while the standing crowd continued to cheer and whistle and clap their hands for what seemed like forever.

Eventually both teams lined up to receive their trophies. First the Yankees, then the Angels, as the loudspeakers delivered "The Impossible Dream." Standing at the end of the Angel line to receive the obligatory handshake of congratulations from Stewart Rand, I suddenly remembered where and when I had last heard that song: while facing the microphone on the bandstand of the Boland town common, waiting to address the huge crowd that had gathered to welcome Sally and Rick and me.

Later, as the shadows were lengthening and I was preparing to leave the field, Timothy came racing over to me, still carrying his trophy. "Mr. Harding, thank you again for everything. My bike. My glove. All your help. I really mean it."

I reached down and picked him up, burying my head in his tiny chest. Shouldn't have done it because I began to sob. "You don't have to thank me, Timothy. I thank you. You've done so much more for me than I've done for you."

"I have?" he asked, obviously puzzled.

"Yes, you have, and I love you."

"I love you, too, Mr. Harding." He held up his trophy. "Thanks to you, I'm now a real champion."

I kissed his cheek and lowered him to the ground. "You've always been a champion, Timothy. Always."

XIV

*A*lthough I was still on a high from our victory, I had no difficulty falling asleep once my head hit the pillow on Saturday night. Certainly I had no plans at all for Sunday, yet on the following morning I awoke shortly after sunrise, showered, shaved, dressed, had a light breakfast and then drove to Maplewood Cemetery, parking the car on a narrow hardtop road just a short walk to Sally and Rick's grave. Fresh grass, recently mowed, already covered their resting-place, but only a short distance away, as a stabbing reminder, was a narrow rectangle of loose gray soil on a fresh gravesite, covered with several faded floral wreaths and baskets containing withered flowers.

I slipped slowly to my knees and then sat back on the grass, hands folded in my lap, as if I were relaxing in a park and waiting for someone to open a picnic basket and begin passing out soft drinks and sandwiches. It was still early, so I was probably the sole human visitor in the cemetery. The only sounds came from several chickadees in a nearby old maple. I closed my eyes, trying to remember prayer words that my mother had taught me long ago. As I said them, haltingly and silently, a blissful peace swept over me, reminiscent of that wonderful feeling of relaxation I would always enjoy whenever I came home late from the office, strung out from pressure until my nerves were at their breaking point, and Sally would insist that I lie on the living-room couch with my head in her lap so that she could caress my temples and forehead with her soft, gentle hands.

With my eyes still closed, I heard myself saying, "Hon, I'm sorry for not coming before now, but I know that you and Rick understand. I just couldn't bring myself to accept the truth—that both your bodies were here, in the ground. But I'm beginning to feel, now, that nearly all my self-pity has just about drained away, that I'm ready to face the world again . . . even . . . even including that job in Concord that was going to mean so much to the three of us and our future. Most of all I think I owe it to the memory of both of you to get on with my life, so will you two please pray for Dad? I'm going to need all the support I can get in the days and weeks ahead."

I rose to my feet and started to walk away before turning to say, softly, "Oh, by the way, I'm sorry there's still no headstone here. No excuse for that. I'll do something about that tomorrow, I promise."

On Monday morning I made two phone calls, which both produced appointments. After spending almost two hours with a patient saleswoman at the Concord Monument Company and finally selecting a very simple red-granite headstone, I had lunch at Millennium Unlimited, in the executive dining room with my good friend, Ralph Manson, who had been functioning in my place as Millennium's acting president. Three other company executives, including Larry Stephenson, chief financial officer, also joined us at my invitation, and everyone seemed actually pleased—shocked and pleased, I guess—to hear my announcement that I was returning to the company.

On the day after Labor Day, thanks to Ralph's tireless cooperation and long hours of meetings, I was back at the helm. Millennium was just about ready to introduce a powerful new word processor software package, called Concord 2000, that our brightest people had been working on long before I had originally joined the company, so the timing of my return was not the best for corporate good. However, everyone just kept smiling as they worked a little harder and a little later each day. Ralph, bless him, was even willing to part with Bette Anton, who had been my secretary and right arm when I joined the company, and she had functioned in that same capacity for Ralph. With Bette's help I managed to survive my first few weeks back on the job, and the long hours didn't bother me at all because now there was nothing to go home for. I probably averaged fifteen-hour days, including Saturdays, until we finally introduced Concord 2000 at a software show in Las Vegas, early in November. It got rave reviews, and I made certain that those who had done so much work on the project were rewarded with promotions and raises, especially Ralph, whom I named my chief operating officer.

One night, following the same routine I had for many weeks, I arrived home shortly after nine, removed the mail from the mailbox, drove up the incline into my garage, made a cup of tea in the kitchen and then walked with teacup, mail and attaché case down the hall into the den, where I would open envelopes, review whatever I had brought home from the office that needed to be read and check my phone messages, if any. This particular night I took a long sip of tea and then tapped the Play button below the slowly blinking red light on my answering machine. The familiar voice of Doc Messenger was saying, "Mr. Harding, sir, you are indeed a difficult man to corral. I've been phoning you for about a week now, and I confess I've been hanging up when your machine comes on. That's no reflection on your message, but my own temerity in dealing with these modern contraptions. However, I have finally decided that what I have to say is important enough for me to risk making a fool of myself with this . . . recording. Sir, it is just a little past seven in the evening as I speak these words, and I beg a favor of you, if you will. Please, no matter what time you return to your home this evening, will you kindly give me a phone call? It is extremely important, or I assure you that I would not be bothering you. My telephone number is 223-4575. I thank you."

"No matter what time you return to your home". . . ? That was enough for me. I dialed his number, and he answered on the first ring.

"Doc, this is John Harding. Just walked in the door and got your message."

"I thank you so very much for returning my call. Now, may I ask another favor of you?"

"Of course."

"I'm certain you have already had a long and grueling day, but how close are you to retiring for the night?"

"Oh, I guess I'm good for about another hour or so."

"Sir, I live just ten minutes away. May I impose on our friendship by asking if I might come visit you to share a matter that I believe you will agree is of great importance? I promise you that I will not take very much of your time."

I stared at the telephone receiver for perhaps ten seconds before replying, "Of course, Doc, come on ahead. I'll put the outside lights on for you."

The line clicked dead. He hadn't even waited to thank me.

Since the front door bell was still out of action, I kept watch out one of the living-room windows until I saw car lights coming up the driveway. Before the old boy could reach for the bell button, I opened the front door and extended my right hand, "Welcome, Doc, come on in."

"Mr. Harding, it's good to see you again."

"Please call me John, Doc."

He smiled and nodded. "I hope all is well at Millennium."

"Well, most of the time I'm not sure. The giant is so huge that keeping all its parts functioning in good health is almost an impossible task, as General Motors and IBM and many others are finally discovering. I guess that nature has been trying to tell us that for centuries. A human who is six feet tall can perform in record fashion in all sorts of endeavors. And yet a human unfortunate enough to be eight feet tall can barely dress and feed himself. Size, in the long run, has very little to do with competency or success."

Doc kept nodding as he walked at my side down the hall to the den. When he entered the room, he looked around admiringly, started to speak and then wisely remained silent. I guess he realized that I needed no more compliments on what a wonderful decorating job my Sally had done. He shook his head when I offered him a drink, and we both sat on the couch that faced out into the now dark backyard. There was no small talk, no talk at all for several minutes while Doc rolled his old hat nervously around in his hands. I thought the smartest thing for me to do was just to sit and remain quiet. I did.

Doc finally leaned forward, his elbows on his knees, frowning as he stared down into the crown of his old headgear. His voice sounded much huskier than usual when he finally began to speak without even glancing in my direction.

"John, I'm afraid I am the bearer of sad news, as if you haven't had enough already to last a lifetime or two. In any event, as you know, little Timothy Noble and his mom have been under my care as a physician ever since they moved here to Boland and Timothy's father departed for warmer climates. Timothy was first brought to me when, according to his mother, he had developed problems with maintaining his balance and occasionally complained of seeing two of everything—double vision. After examining the young man twice I decided, with his mother's approval, that a few of my colleagues at the Dartmouth-Hitchcock Medical Center should take a look at him. They put Timothy through a long series of tests."

Doc suddenly stood, facing away from me. I had a sudden urge to jump up and run out of the room. I didn't want to hear anymore!

"John, they discovered that Timothy has a brain tumor, and because of its unusual position it is inoperable. *Medulla blastoma* is one of the more exotic medical names for the damn thing. We considered chemotherapy for a while, but smarter heads than mine finally convinced us that, because of the tumor's location, we had little or no chance of inducing any sort of remission for any worthwhile length of time. So the decision was made by his mother, after several very difficult discussions with me, to allow Timothy to continue his normal day-to-day schedule like any other child his age as long as he could. That pleased Timothy very much, of course, except that the young man hung a condition on things.

He made both of us promise that we would tell no one about his problem. He said he didn't want anyone, especially his school friends, feeling sorry for him and giving him special breaks because they knew he was soon going to die. He wanted to be treated just like every other eleven-year-old."

I had heard Doc's words clearly. I had understood exactly what Doc had said. And yet . . . and yet, I found myself saying, "Doc, are you telling me that Timothy knew that his life was doomed, that he was going to die? He knew it?"

"He did. His mother, Peggy, is a special and tough little lady. As I said, the two of us had several talks before she made the decision that Timothy deserved to know. I distinctly remember the evening when, with tears running down her cheeks, she said that if God had decided that she could only have her baby for eleven or maybe twelve years, then the very least she could do was to tell the boy the truth so that he would be able to at least try to handle the gift of each new day as he wanted to handle it."

I caught myself raising my voice. I apologized. Then I said, "Doc, this whole baseball season. You saw it. That kid never stopped hustling. He never stopped trying and he was always cheering for his teammates. Remember 'Day by day, in every way' and 'Never, never, never give up'? God only knows how much he meant to the Angels. Are you telling me that little boy played and acted the way he did, with enthusiasm, hustle, drive, cheers and smiles, always encouraging the other kids, even though he knew ... even though he knew he was soon going to die?"

Doc stared down at the floor and slowly nodded his head.

"And it was okay for him to play?"

"I thought it would be good for him, when he asked me in the presence of his mother, since no possible additional harm could come from playing and it would help keep his mind on other things. Playing, if anything, I believed, might help lengthen his term of mobility."

"I haven't seen him for more than three months, Doc. How is he?"

"Well, these days he has to work a lot harder to keep a smile on his face, since he's now in constant pain, has a hell of a time keeping his balance and about the only way he can get around is in his wheelchair. However, there isn't very much area to cover in that little home of theirs, so he manages okay."

"What about his mother?"

"Well, she quit her job and stays close by his side. His school sent home books and stuff for a while, but she couldn't handle that, so she feeds him and keeps him clean and just tries to be a companion. She told me this morning that he's sleeping a lot of the time now, and when he isn't, he tries to read and watches a little television."

"If she's not working, Doc, how are they getting by? Is there any money?"

He shook his head, still avoiding my eyes. "There's

none. I'm helping out some. At my age I don't have anyone else to worry about or spend it on anyway."

Doc finally sat down again, now closer to me. I reached out and placed my hand on his shoulder. "How about a hospital? Would Timothy be better off there?"

"I don't believe so. Not yet, anyway. Be it ever so humble, I think he's better off in his own home and his own bed. Special hospital facilities and equipment can do very little to relieve his condition, and Peggy has no group hospital insurance. We've just got to keep him comfortable as long as possible."

"Doc, what can I do?"

The old man smiled faintly and said, "I was hoping that you would ask. The best thing you can do, John, is pay the little guy a visit. He's still constantly talking about his base hit and how Mr. Harding taught him the right way to hold a bat and swing. Do you know what he sleeps with?"

"What?"

"The baseball glove you gave him."

On the following morning I phoned Bette at the office, telling her I'd be two or three hours late. She reminded me that I was having lunch with a couple of editors from the magazine *Macworld* at noon, and said she'd hold down the fort until I got there. I drove down to the bank and withdrew a thousand dollars in twenties, waved to Stewart Rand in his office and got out of the building before he could corner me in a long and meaningless conversation. Then I went into Jerry's Bike and Toy Shop, next to the bank, and bought the complete boxed set of Topps Major League baseball cards for the two previous years. Jerry's wife was nice enough to gift wrap them for me.

A light rain was falling when I finally arrived at the gray mailbox with NOBLE painted on the side in uneven streaks. I turned on the muddy road, just beyond, and drove up close to the front door. Peggy Noble must have seen or heard my car approaching, because the door opened before I had a chance to knock. She was standing in the doorway, in an old green warm-up suit, touching her protruding right forefinger again and again against her pursed lips in a signal for me not to speak. Slowly she closed the door behind me and whispered, "I'm so glad you came. Timothy dozed off a little while ago while watching some cartoons on television."

I turned toward the old black-and-white television set. Not far away from it was a wheelchair, and in it was Timothy, his head tilted back, mouth partially open, sound asleep. I moved closer to the chair and knelt down so that I could get a better look at him. While I was staring at his small handsome face, his eyes suddenly opened wide. He immediately leaned forward with both arms reaching toward me.

"Mr. Harding, you came to see me! Wow! Mom, look, Mr. Harding is here!"

"Yes, I know. Isn't that nice, dear?"

I couldn't help myself. I leaned forward, wrapped my

arms around him and kissed his cheek, then his forehead. He returned my kisses with both his arms around
my neck.

"I knew you would come. I knew it! I knew it!"

I wiped at my face with the palms of my hands and
handed him the two gift-wrapped boxes, which he immediately opened. "Oh, wow! Mom, look! Baseball
cards! Hundreds of them! Neat! Here's Bobby Bonds and
here is . . . Wade Boggs! Wow! Thank you, Mr. Harding.
Thank you."

"Timothy, I would have come to see you before, but
I didn't even know you were sick. Honest. I've been
working in Concord . . . long days . . . so I never knew
until Doc Messenger told me."

"Did he tell you that I was going to die?"

I didn't know how to respond. Finally I just nodded.

He ran his tiny fingers through his blond hair and
grinned. "But I got my wish, Mr. Harding. I prayed to
God, you know. I asked God to let me play the whole
schedule of games and get a hit, and I did . . . I did,
thanks to you . . . and . . . and God."

He reached under the blanket that covered the lower
part of his body and held up his baseball glove. Then,
as suddenly as he had awakened, his energy seemed to
drain away and his eyes began to close. Within minutes
he was sound asleep. I patted his arm, turned, and went
over to his mother, who had been patiently sitting at
the kitchen table, having left Timothy and I to our
"men" talk.

"Would you like a cup of coffee, Mr. Harding? I just made a pot."

"I'd love a cup. Thanks."

Sitting next to her, in that tiny kitchen, I felt so helpless. Then I remembered, reached into my inside jacket pocket and removed the brown envelope with the money. I slid it across the table toward Mrs. Noble, reached out for her hand, grasped it and placed it on top of the envelope.

"What's this?" she asked.

I held her hand. "Just call it a little unemployment compensation, okay? Now, don't say anything, please."

I then reached back inside my jacket, removed my personal checkbook and ballpoint pen and wrote out a check to her. "And I would like you to use this, as you wish, so that you and Timothy can get whatever you need. Also," I said, removing one of my business cards from my wallet and scribbling on the back, "here is my home phone number. You need anything, you call me, promise? The office number is on the front, and I'll make arrangements so that if you phone me there, the call will get right through to me."

She just sat and stared at me, shaking her head, looking completely confused. "Why are you doing all this for us? You hardly know us, Mr. Harding."

"Mrs. Noble . . ."

"Peggy, please."

"Peggy, when that little boy of yours came into my life, early this summer, I was about ready to end it.

Without my wife and son I had absolutely no desire to go on living. My life had no value at all to me, but Timothy's courage and soaring spirit penetrated my blackest moments of despair, picked me up, brushed me off, taught me how to smile again, reminded me to count my blessings and encouraged me to deal with each day, one at a time. Timothy's struggle on the diamond reminded me of the miracles any of us can accomplish when we refuse to give up. That little boy taught me how to live again. What's my life worth? How can I put a price on Timothy's salvage work? How could I possibly repay him for the candle he lit in my life? What price?"

I buried my head in my hands.

"Mr. Harding, sir . . . ?"

Timothy had awakened. I rose, walked over to him and sat on the floor, next to the wheelchair. "Yes, Timothy?"

"Do you pray for your little boy?"

"I sure do."

"Will you pray for me, too, when I'm dead?"

"Every time I pray for Rick, I'll pray for you too."

He nodded and smiled. "And as long as I'm here, will you still come to see me?"

"I promise."

And I kept my promise, several times each week, even including Thanksgiving . . . and Christmas . . . and New Year's . . . and Valentine's Day. . . .

X V

Timothy Noble died on April 7th.

He was buried in a plot not far from Sally and Rick.

As I had promised, one day I drove Peggy Noble to consult with the helpful saleslady at the monument company. Although I had told her that she was free to pick out any stone and size she wanted for Timothy, she finally selected a piece of dark-gray granite in the shape of a small obelisk, on which she had engraved:

TIMOTHY NOBLE
March 12, 1979   April 7, 1991
I never, never, never gave up!

On Memorial Day, early in the afternoon, I visited Maplewood Cemetery and lovingly placed a wicker basket of pink Simplicity roses close to the red stone marking Sally and Rick's resting-place. After several prayers I remained on my knees for I don't know how long before I finally rose and walked slowly to Timothy Noble's grave. I knelt near the side of his gray stone, close enough to touch it, and removed from a paper bag the baseball glove I had given Timothy. At my request his mother had returned it to me, a few hours ago, without any questions. Now I placed it at the front of the stone with the base of the glove spread widely so that it stood balanced on the grass with its leather fingers pointed upward as if they were reaching for heaven with a small hand still inside.

"Thank you, little guy, for being *my* angel of hope and courage. I'll always love you, and every time I take a breath, I owe you a little more."

Sometime during the warm days of summer baseball, three years hence, the township of Boland will celebrate their opening of a new public library. All the arrangements have been finalized for it to be erected on the site of the old one that was destroyed by fire. I have already taken care of all the financial details.

The library will be called the Harding-Noble Public Library—and in its carpeted foyer will hang separate oil paintings . . .

. . . paintings of two little boys.

ABOUT THE AUTHOR

Og Mandino is the most widely read inspirational and self-help author in the world today. His fifteen books have sold more than twenty-five million copies in twenty languages. Thousands of people from all walks of life have openly credited Og Mandino with turning their lives around and for the miracle they have found in his words. His books of wisdom, inspiration, and love include *The Greatest Salesman in the World; The Greatest Salesman in the World, Part II: The End of the Story; The Christ Commission; The Greatest Secret in the World; Og Mandino's University of Success; Mission: Success!; A Better Way to Live;* and *The Return of the Ragpicker.*